LOYAL To A FAULT

LOYAL TO A FAULT

How to Establish New Patterns When Loving Others Has Left You Hurting

Courtney J. Burg

W PUBLISHING GROUP

AN IMPRINT OF THOMAS NELSON

Published in Nashville, Tennessee, by W Publishing, an imprint of Thomas Nelson.

Thomas Nelson titles may be purchased in bulk for educational, business, fundraising, or sales promotional use. For information, please email SpecialMarkets@ThomasNelson.com.

Unless otherwise noted, Scripture quotations are taken from The Holy Bible, New International Version®, NIV®. Copyright © 1973, 1978, 1984, 2011 by Biblica, Inc.® Used by permission of Zondervan. All rights reserved worldwide. www.Zondervan.com. The "NIV" and "New International Version" are trademarks registered in the United States Patent and Trademark Office by Biblica, Inc.®

Scripture quotations marked NKJV are taken from the New King James Version®. Copyright © 1982 by Thomas Nelson. Used by permission. All rights reserved.

Scripture quotations marked NLT are taken from the Holy Bible, New Living Translation. © 1996, 2004, 2015 by Tyndale House Foundation. Used by permission of Tyndale House Publishers, Inc., Carol Stream, Illinois 60188. All rights reserved.

Any internet addresses, phone numbers, or company or product information printed in this book are offered as a resource and are not intended in any way to be or to imply an endorsement by Thomas Nelson, nor does Thomas Nelson vouch for the existence, content, or services of these sites, phone numbers, companies, or products beyond the life of this book.

ISBN 978-1-4003-3587-9 (audiobook)
ISBN 978-1-4003-3586-2 (ePub)
ISBN 978-1-4003-3585-5 (TP)

Library of Congress Control Number: 2023938170

Printed in the United States of America
23 24 25 26 27 LBC 5 4 3 2 1

To my parents: it wasn't your fault. To my four children: it isn't yours to carry. To God: thank you for turning beauty from ashes, always. May I represent you well.

Contents

CONTENTS

PART 3: LEGACY WRITING

Introduction

I KNEW ABOUT GOD AT A VERY YOUNG AGE BUT
never felt close to him. I grew up in an Irish Catholic home, where I
was encouraged to memorize prayers, participate in Mass, and repent
of my sins. I loved going to Sunday school and dressing up for Easter
and Christmas, yet as I got older, the Savior I understood felt distant
and cold.

I was taught to place family over everything—sometimes, it
seemed, even over God. This meant pretending that the addiction,
dysfunction, and chaos that was happening inside our home actually
wasn't—because a good Christian girl remained loyal to her family,
regardless of the cost. Later in life this would become the source of my
greatest inner conflict, as the patterns of behavior I heavily relied on as
a child would slowly wreak havoc on my adult relationships, not just
as a daughter and sister but as a wife, mother, coworker, and friend.

I had spent decades chasing approval, security, and my identity
in all the wrong people and places. I had grown so consumed by the
feelings and expectations of those around me that I lived daily with
shame and anxiety, shattering myself into pieces trying to keep others
around me whole. Until, one day, I was forced to choose.

I was newly married when my husband returned home from work

one morning after forgetting something, only to find me in bed drinking whiskey out of a coffee mug. It was then that I realized I had to stop praying, begging, and pleading with God to help me fix, save, and rescue everyone else I loved to no avail. *I had to start fixing myself.*

I was done warping into different roles—caretaker, perfectionist, people pleaser, and performer—just to be accepted. I was sick of betraying myself, giving until there was nothing left to give, then feeling hurt, taken advantage of, and resentful. I was through justifying others' mistreatment of me and my mistreatment of myself because I didn't know how to be in relationship any other way. And I was finished lying to myself about just how out of control my life had become.

I did not know what codependency meant, and I certainly had no idea what a boundary was. I only knew I could no longer keep loving others the way I had been, when doing so continuously left me hurting. I began to challenge what it meant to be loyal, and with the help of my husband, my sponsor, a therapist, and a new unearthed relationship with God, I started learning and implementing new patterns of behavior inside my relationships.

By putting in the work, I have been able to break free from the limiting beliefs I inherited around what it means to be a loving woman. I began boundary setting to guard the new values I had created for myself, and I no longer allowed guilt, insecurity, or fear of abandonment to dictate my every move. I stopped allowing others' anger, unhealed wounds, and expectations to control me, and I began living with an eternal perspective instead of the convenient, familiar, earthly one I had always known.

I made a choice to no longer be a victim to my biology or circumstances. Instead, I started taking authority over my thoughts and behaviors, rebuking strongholds, and intentionally claiming the legacy I hope to one day leave my four children. And one of my greatest pleasures of late is that I can support other women through this same process in my online coaching community, Discover Your Worth.

If you aren't sure what is next for you, that's okay—you don't have to know. But if you sense that God has more in store for you than what you are settling for right now, I want to confirm and declare over you today: he is good, his promises keep, and it isn't too late for you. There is so much hope and redemption in this life to be had, and you are worthy of it all, not because others say so, and certainly not because you have earned it, but because you are redeemed by the precious blood of Jesus.

Bold steps must be taken to reclaim what God says is true about you and to challenge what isn't. By the grace of God alone, I no longer live loyal to a fault in my relationships, and this is my hope for you. It wasn't easy and it did not come naturally, but thankfully for us all, God left us much instruction. It is my prayer that this book points you back to the way he intended you to love, even when it's messy, and especially when it's hard.

PART 1

How Did We Get Here?

MANY WOMEN WERE RAISED INSIDE dysfunctional homes. For whatever reason, their childhoods were lost or stolen as they were asked to care for others at the cost of losing themselves. Maybe you are one of these women, and you are now living with the consequences of this deprivation in your adult relationships. Whether by default or desperation, you took on a role as caregiver and now feel unskilled at caring for yourself in the way God asks you to. Your relationships suffer, and so does your mental well-being, and perhaps you are wondering, *Is this all there is?*

I want to encourage you: it isn't. What God has in store for you is so much better than what he will be asking you to leave behind. To learn new healthy patterns of behavior, I suggest that you approach this first section as an opportunity to acknowledge the unhealthy patterns that may be present in your relationships today. Allow both curiosity and grace to be your close friends, as some of what you discover in these pages may be revealed to you for the very first time. It is my hope that God will guide you toward learning how to tend to what is yours through letting go of what isn't.

1

Keeping Everything Together

I GREW UP THE YOUNGEST OF THREE CHILDREN IN a hardworking middle-class family. My father did maintenance at a nearby hospital; he was a man of both resilience and grit. His parents died when he was just a boy, so he was used to a life of deprivation and fending for himself.

My mother worked the register at the local drugstore. As she was the second oldest of seven siblings, much of her life was spent caring for others. She, too, knew how to live without.

I was raised in an Irish Catholic home and knew of God as a young child, but I did not *know* him. The Scripture I heard the priest recite on Sundays did not negate the confusion I carried inside. I was taught that honoring God meant to honor my family, even if some of what we were doing together was far from honorable. My faith would slowly become both a blessing and a burden. If God loved me so much, then why would my life at home feel so heavy?

As a child, I felt as if I were the glue keeping everything together. I would override the nudge that this wasn't my role, because in a lot of ways I enjoyed and needed it. I loved what we had and never envied what we didn't. And while it seemed as though we lived double lives, behaving at home in ways vastly different from how we did in public, this felt normal. To the standards of family culture today, maybe it was.

My parents had good intentions. My mom and dad did, and continue to do, the best they can with what they have and with what they knew. They far exceeded what they each received as a child growing up, and for that I am grateful. It wouldn't be until much later in life, however, that I would understand that when people are sinned against, they often use similar sin to cope.

> **When people are sinned against, they often use similar sin to cope.**

I have two older brothers who navigated homelife in their own ways, often with alcohol or drugs. They dropped out of school as teens, falling quickly and consistently into trouble with the law. For me, I coped through pretending. If I could pretend our home wasn't riddled with addiction, and if I could pretend that the fighting between my parents wasn't happening, then I could continue pretending that I wasn't worried or scared that it was. I never wanted to add to the mess or problems, so I chose to smile through it, excelling in both academics and athletics. I believed that this pretending reflected my love and devotion for them and our family. I even found ways to be helpful and productive, which often meant abandoning my own needs and feelings. This pattern of behavior was both modeled and rewarded and is how the seed of codependency took root.

Maybe you can relate to some degree. Perhaps you didn't experience the consequences of addiction, but you took on a role as caretaker, provider, or people pleaser, a job that was never yours to fill. This allowed you to maintain a connection to those you couldn't imagine living life without. Yet, by doing so, you had certain needs go unmet, and over time their deprivation became yours. Slowly, in your search for distraction to cope, this deprivation made you do things and become things you weren't designed by God to ever do or become.

DISTRACTIONS

It wasn't until I hit my late teens that I realized remaining loyal to my bloodline also meant remaining loyal to our secrets, wounds, and suffering, although I could not (and would not) articulate this until decades later. I did, however, agree within myself to the sacrifice, regardless of its price, because it was one I was willing to pay to stay connected to those I loved the most.

My mother brought me and my two older brothers to church consistently as children, but surrendering to a loving God often felt punitive. Somewhere deep down I knew that following God would mean I would have to turn my back on the sin eroding our family, which would result in turning my back on the only family I ever knew. It would be a battle, a war I would one day have to wage. But I wouldn't be ready for a long while, not until the pain of staying the same began to surpass the pain of making change. Going to hell never felt so scary as long as we were headed there together.

I have lots of fond memories as a child growing up in South Florida. Most Saturdays were spent on the soccer fields, with my father serving as my youth coach for many seasons. Every goal I ever scored, my mom would sew a soccer patch onto my athletic shorts, which still brings me joy to this day. Sundays after church we would head down to the beach—lugging our bagged sandwiches and boogie boards onto the sand. And holidays were always picture-perfect; decorations were hung and home-cooked meals always served.

But I have some unpleasant memories too. The cops being called because my brother punched a hole in the wall, again. My mom pulling the car over so Dad could puke on the side of the road after one too many brews. Fighting, crying, and confusion that left me at night filled with more questions than answers. I was always surrounded by people, yet at times I felt utterly afraid and alone. Try as I may, these don't depart my memory. The good doesn't erase the bad.

As I matured, I would often ask myself, *Am I making this up?*
Am I being overly sensitive?
Am I being too dramatic?
I have since learned that I was not.

———

Perhaps your childhood didn't look like mine, but for whatever reason, you felt a similar deprivation and confusion. When children are young, they have a need to trust their caregivers for more than just the essentials, like food in the fridge or a solid roof overhead. There are emotional needs that must be met too. Trust is not something that happens automatically through genetics, nor is it a onetime event that seals the deal. It is a slow process that includes consistency and predictability. Children need to be reassured that when life gets confusing, there is someone they can trust who can help make sense of the chaos. They need an adult who can look them in the eye and have honest, age-appropriate, sometimes difficult conversations about life, about love, about loss.

When a child feels safe, she can learn, connect, self-regulate, explore, and so much more. From this space of safety, she is better equipped to face life's challenges and setbacks with confidence and clarity.

But many adult women today suffer from a lack of self-trust, as we tend to repeat what we don't repair. When you are raised around chaos and dysfunction, even briefly or suddenly, you look to the adults around you for reassurance. You look to see if they, too, notice the chaos and dysfunction. If they don't, you slowly turn inward. Instead of questioning the people around you, you begin to question *yourself*. You internalize the problem as "me."

Maybe I am wrong.

Maybe I am overreacting.

Maybe I am to blame.

Maybe I am the mistake.

There are many ways children can be altered by their family of origin, but these wounds, when left unhealed, create patterns of behavior that leave us craving, searching, and working to earn love. The coping begins, and the most common way to cope with this pain is through distractions.

Distractions become an unsafe child's best friend. When the world is crumbling around her, any distraction becomes her constant. It's predictable. It's a manufactured safety. It's something she can trust because it is something she can control.

The most common distraction for children who are raised in dysfunction is parenting their own parents or raising their own siblings. I took to this swiftly, becoming therapist to my parents in their marital affairs, or holding my brother as he lay on the couch after a near overdose. Somewhere inside I knew it wasn't my job, but I loved my family and wanted to help, even if it meant pushing aside what *I* needed.

It's something she can trust because it is something she can control.

Whether a caregiver consciously offers up this role, or the role is tossed into a child's lap by default, a child thrives here because it keeps her busy and distracted, helps her feel useful, and in a lot of ways secures the very connection she desperately craves.

Unfortunately for many, this behavior isn't left in childhood.

Distractions are at the core of why many adult women spend their lives people-pleasing, performing, and pretending. They strive to stay busy, running themselves into the ground and even attempting to rescue or fix others to somehow fix themselves. They numb, avoid, and hide to try to bandage up the internal discomfort. They, like me and perhaps even you, were never taught how to deal with the chaos, the turmoil, the dysfunction, but rather were well practiced in how not to deal with it.

But you and I were created for more.

Yes, deprivation can leave us all seeking out various distractions to cope. But this very same deprivation can be used to our advantage. Deprivation turned to desperation can become the very conduit that leads you back to God. After all, he is the only one who can turn emptiness into fullness if we let him.

We were created for connection. From the beginning of time, our Creator wired us this way. We see it in Genesis when God said, "It is not good for the man to be alone. I will make a helper suitable for him" (2:18).

God did not want us to be alone. He literally created us to be in relationship with him and one another. He designed us for our marriages, family, and friendships. He wanted us to learn from our peers, to celebrate and mourn together, and to grow in community and fellowship. This was a part of his plan and design. And when done the way he asks us to, it brings him (and us) much pleasure. So what happened that made us become so loyal to a fault?

DECEPTION

Satan also had a plan. Once he heard that God wanted to create a man to inhabit his once formless world, Satan knew he would lose some power and authority, and this made him rebellious. He was exiled from heaven, and you know what happened next—Adam and Eve fell for his temptation. This original sin now infiltrates humanity and our most tender relationships.

I find it hard to believe that one of God's most loyal archangels turned his back on his very Creator in pursuit of power. I would imagine that heaven was perfect, and that Lucifer (in his pre-Satan days) had anything and everything he needed to live a cozy, comfortable life. But in his discontentment he lost sight of his Creator and chose to trade eternity for a life of sin.

Sin causes us to worship creation over our Creator, and perhaps our most favorite creation is each other. When we don't stick to God's original plan, when we fail to remain obedient to his limitations, when we try to do the work only God can do by trying to fix, heal, or save others, we find ourselves abusing his creation at our very own expense. It is no wonder, then, why some of our closest relationships reflect hell more than heaven.

So how do we get right with God again? How do we guard ourselves from the temptation of rescuing those we care about? How do we dwell in our relationships with healthy limits, confidence, and clarity?

> **Sin causes us to worship creation over our Creator, and perhaps our most favorite creation is each other.**

I really do believe most of us want to love others well. We want the relationships God intended for us to have. We crave the enjoyment that comes through this authentic connection with one another. And maybe for a while, with select people, we do find that. We feel safe, seen, and understood. Yet it is only a matter of time before we find ourselves doing it again.

Again, I tried to help you, and you didn't even thank me.

Again, I lied for you, and you still aren't getting sober.

Again, I pretended like this wasn't happening, but it is, and I feel trapped.

Again, I swore this would be the last time, but here we are.

Again, I believed if I just stuck around longer, it would get better.

Where does all this brokenness even come from? We read in Genesis that the fall of mankind came when Adam and Eve were tempted by Satan in snake form and took fruit from the forbidden tree. Why would God even place a tree in the garden for the Enemy to use at all? I mean, it seems like it would be an easy thing to avoid altogether, right? Reading through some commentary, I found this:

> Not everything that *can* be done *should* be done. Human imagination and skill can work with the resources of God's creation in ways inimical [harmful] to God's intents, purposes, and commands. If we want to work *with* God, rather than *against* him, we must choose to observe the limits God sets, rather than realizing everything possible in creation.[1]

Yes, God created the tree. But he also gave us the power to choose.

If we want to work with God, we must choose.

If we want to dwell inside safe, reciprocal relationships, we must choose.

If we want to turn away from sin, we must choose.

If we want to bear much fruit, we must choose.

If we want to experience the satisfaction and joy that God has for us in our relationships, we must choose.

And here we find the answer to his perfect love. We are to love him well through choosing to pursue, honor, and trust him first. This takes obeying his commands, seeking his will over our own, and worshiping him over any of his other creations. It takes honoring the limits he places on our lives, including how we choose to love one another.

But we still have the tree. And all our "agains." And the never-ending temptation to rescue, save, and fix everyone . . . so what's a girl to do, really? Because if you are anything like me, you need to hear it straight. You're thinking, *Give me some practical tips and tools that I can apply right away*, right? I have them, and they are coming.

But the takeaway for now is this: we've got to discern the deception.

The biggest tactic the Enemy uses is deception. His favorite way of using deception is through getting you to believe a lie that feels familiar and personal, because he knows this is how he can get you hiding from God and, eventually, distant and disconnected from others.

> We are to love him well through choosing to pursue, honor, and trust him first.

It doesn't look this way, of course.

The word *satan* is the English transliteration of a Hebrew word for "adversary" in the Bible.[2] If the Enemy is our adversary, his primary goal is to tear you away from your Creator. And you'd better believe he isn't foolish enough to let you see him coming.

The good news is that patterns repeat themselves, and we have a long line of history throughout the Bible to pull from that helps pinpoint his attack. In one encounter with Jesus, we see the Enemy's tactics plain as day. Let's dive into that story.

FORTY DAYS IN THE WILDERNESS

There is so much to glean from the Gospel of Matthew and its portrait of Jesus, his healing work, and his teachings. But let us not rush past these verses that give clear insight into the devil and his tactics of deception. We read about how Jesus withdrew to the wilderness to fast and pray for forty days shortly before his own ministry began, when Satan showed up to tempt him.

Challenge

In Matthew 4, we read that the devil said to Jesus, "If you are the Son of God, tell these stones to become bread" (v. 3).

If.

He isn't just tempting Jesus to miraculously make bread from stone, because Jesus could do so if he wanted to. And he isn't just tempting Jesus to satisfy his physical appetite. No, it goes much deeper than that. He is challenging Jesus' *identity*. The Enemy knows that if he can trip up your spiritual footing, and if he can convince you into thinking you can satisfy your own needs without God, then he can sever your dependence on him. As Spurgeon said, "He bids the Lord prove his Sonship by catering for himself; and yet that would have been the surest way to prove that he was not the Son of God."[3]

For us today, it may sound more like this: "If you are a loyal daughter . . . you would keep this secret."

"If you are a dedicated mother . . . you would pay his rent."

"If you are a good friend . . . you would help her."

"If you are a Christian . . . you would remain loyal, no matter the cost."

Satan may use old mistakes, shame, or current strongholds to keep you from claiming your rightful position as a child of God. He may twist the truth just so, in a way that has you doubting God's provisions and your place. He may have you considering that God has forgotten you, left you, and that you must survive on your own or else you won't survive at all. He may have you going to bed at night worrying that if you don't prove your love or hustle to keep that relationship intact, then they won't stay, and you'll be left alone. He does this because he knows if you can't remember whom you belong to, you become a free agent, and he can then convince you that you are his.

Confuse

We see the devil bring Jesus to the pinnacle of the temple, where he told him to throw himself off the edge to prove that the angels would catch him. He then proceeded to use Scripture (Ps. 91:11–12) to persuade Jesus:

> For he will command his angels concerning you to guard you in all your ways; they will lift you up in their hands, so that you will not strike your foot against a stone.

Notice that the Enemy created this manufactured crisis, an illustration of urgency doused in fear. But he didn't stop there; he offered comfort and reassurance to the Son of God himself. He took an out-of-context scripture and contorted its intended meaning, trying to confuse Jesus into using the power bestowed on him to command the angels for protection and saving. Again, Jesus could have done this if he had chosen to. But he remained obedient. He guarded himself and withstood the temptation. He saw the bigger picture.

Just consider for a moment—if the Enemy is bold enough to tempt God's Son with the very words of God, why would we be any exception?

Anytime I am tempted to believe a lie about what it means to be loyal to those I love, if I pause ever so briefly, I will notice it is a situation that appears both urgent and alluring. But here is the deal: authentic loyalty is never urgent or alluring.

Take for example the time I lent my brother rent money. I knew he had been recently fired from his job, and I also knew his car had just been repossessed. But I didn't pause to consider how his own actions

> **If the Enemy is bold enough to tempt God's Son with the very words of God, why would we be any exception?**

brought on those consequences. Instead, I dropped everything I was doing to scramble together what little cash I had to lend him, trying to keep a roof over his head. To no one's surprise, he did not use the money for rent, nor did he pay me back, and I was left in a pinch with my own bills. I had allowed his problem to become mine.

Looking back, I see how I had believed a lie about what a loyal sister was. I also allowed the fear of losing my brother's approval or affection to dictate my actions. Because his problem seemed urgent, and because I wanted to be the hero in this story, I responded hastily. This is the confusion and reinforcement that leaves relationships at high risk for pain, hurt, and continued dysfunction.

Befriend

In one final attempt, the Enemy tried to offer partial power through allegiance. "'All this I will give you,' he said, 'if you will bow down and worship me'" (Matt. 4:9).

Jesus was feeling hungry, tired, and alone. And after Jesus had fended off all the temptations leading up to this, the Enemy's last ploy was to soften his approach and offer a vision and partnership into a future they could have together—he promised to give him land and power.

It's as if he were saying, as he wrapped his arm around the neck of Jesus, "Look at all we could have, just you and me."

All he needed was Jesus to agree.

To his promises.

To his future.

To his deception.

We are told "the thief comes only to steal and kill and destroy" (John 10:10), and he can use various forms of deception to get his way. After all, he is the prince of evil spirits, the enemy of God, who is roaming the earth disguised as an angel of light.[4]

But it isn't enough to live life on guard. We must understand where he receives inspiration for his creative tactics. You see, the Enemy knows that if he can offer us the desires of our flesh and fulfill our natural appetites for identity, meaning, and connection, we will be more likely to take the bait. In James 1:14 we can quickly gain understanding: "But each person is tempted when they are dragged away by *their own* evil desire and enticed" (emphasis added).

Aren't sure what your own desires are? Well, consider my example from before when I helped my brother with his rent. Looking back, I see that I was in a pretty bad spot myself. My boyfriend and I had just broken up, and I was feeling insecure and unloved. My brother's problem presented itself at a time when I was vulnerable. (Coincidence? I think not.) Out of desperation I saw his problem as an opportunity to heal my own loneliness. The problem is that you can never fix a problem with a problem. Anything that has you responding impulsively, or without self-control, is never from God. Remember, God isn't in a hurry, and if we are to become more like him, we have to start here.

Loving others through losing the best of who God created you to be isn't love at all. Yet Satan will do his very best to distract, deceive, and confuse us all into thinking so, and this is how we find ourselves in a mess. For a long time, I feared that if I didn't earn love or prove my worth to others, they would leave me. But I wouldn't be able to confront this fear until I began to challenge the unhealthy patterns of connecting that I had grown accustomed to.

ACKNOWLEDGE & CONFRONT

1. Did you take on a role (people pleaser, caretaker, etc.) that wasn't yours out of deprivation as a child? Describe that role. Is this a role you are still playing in your adult relationships? How so?

2. How does distracting yourself with other people's problems allow you to feel in control and safe?

3. Has Satan deceived you into worshiping someone else over God? How has this affected your well-being and ability to show up healthy inside relationships (with yourself and others)?

4. What lies are you believing and acting on that leave you losing yourself in your relationships (e.g., *If I am a loyal daughter/friend/sister/mother, I should . . .*)?

5. In what way is this lie feeding your flesh's desire for identity, meaning, or connection (e.g., by becoming the hero in the story)?

2

Dirty Laundry

I LAY THERE WITH MY HANDS OVER MY EARS, trying to block out the yelling I heard through the walls. I knew it would pass—it always did—but I would have to wait. I curled myself up inside the sheets of my twin daybed, its white vintage frame pressed beneath the windowsill that looked out at the large oak tree in my front yard.

As a child, I was scared by the yelling. I waited for the next loud *thump*—a body being thrown against a wall. It felt like the whole house was shaking. My teenage brothers and my father exchanging profanities. My mother screaming. Doors would slam. Then it would get quiet. Always followed by my mother's tears.

I didn't understand why it always had to come to this. I don't think they did either. Most days everything was fine. Everyone getting along, aside from some small annoyances, irritations . . . typical friction among five family members living in a small home. I loved my life; I just didn't love this part of it.

I knew a substance was to blame. I heard my mother complain

about it. I saw the way she looked at my dad when he opened another can of beer, or the disgust and disappointment that would infuse the room when either of my brothers came home high. I could sense the shift happen; very few words needed to be exchanged to feel the tension building. It became rhythmic in a way, but never predictable. I didn't know when it would be coming; I just knew it always would.

The explosions.

The hurtful words.

The couch turned on its side.

The isolation and hurt.

How could people behave a certain way in public and then be so barbaric behind closed doors? It was all so confusing.

I was around eight years old when I first understood that remaining loyal to my family really meant keeping secrets. A fight broke out one evening, just before dusk, and in a panic I sprinted three doors down to a neighbor's house to ask for help, my little fists beating against her front door, my heart racing. I stood there waiting, barefoot, when the small, elderly woman came to the screen enclosure to greet me.

Remaining loyal to my family really meant keeping secrets.

"Call the cops!" I said, shaking and out of breath. But before she could get to her landline, I felt my mother's hand on my shoulder. "Sweetie, come home. Everything is okay." She nodded to the woman, reassuring her, "My boys just got into a little scuffle."

That's always what these things were to us. Little. Insignificant. Normal. And I lived with this skewed belief for a very long time. I would eventually even learn how to defend and justify it all, to others and, of course, to myself. I knew families had disagreements. I also knew that it was impossible for everyone to get along all the time.

But this was a part of our hardwiring, and as I got older, I began to understand just how much this unhealthy behavior kept us connected.

COMMON-ENEMY INTIMACY

Common-enemy intimacy is a term I first heard from researcher and social scientist Dr. Brené Brown. She shares how we can form a loyalty and bond with each other through the hating of someone or something together. This form of intimacy is one that is "often intense, immediately gratifying, and an easy way to discharge outrage and pain. It is not, however, fuel for real connection."[1] The problem with this sort of connection is that it is counterfeit. It is a false way to feel temporarily seen and understood, without having to do the messy work it takes to show up authentically and honestly in our relationships.

It can be difficult to become aware of this pattern of connection, especially if common-enemy intimacy is deeply ingrained and habitual in nature. It can be easily justified or minimized by those who share it, which only adds to its destructive power. I didn't know this was how I searched for and secured connection in my relationships until I was humbly confronted by a friend about it.

I had pulled into the garage of my house and put the car in Park. I was newly engaged and on the phone chatting with my best friend, Allison, whom I had known since high school.

"Gosh, Alli, I still can't believe she did that! You know, I wouldn't wear that out if I were her. It's a little too much, don't you think?" I said.

"Well, I don't know. That's not up to me. And, in fact, I have decided not to talk about other people anymore. Gossiping just doesn't feel good to me like it used to," she replied.

My heart sank as I slid down in my seat. I felt a combination of both embarrassment and shame. Never had anyone ever *not* gossiped with me, let alone confronted me head-on like that. It was foreign, weird, and uncomfortable to be shut down.

And then something else happened. I was genuinely speechless. In fact, in the days and weeks that followed, I found myself not actually knowing how to chat with girlfriends without bad-mouthing someone else. It was as if that was the only way I knew how to connect.

I would later learn that this was very much like the common-enemy intimacy Dr. Brené Brown referred to. It was a habit of connecting that I'd picked up on in childhood, which usually included some form of gossiping, passive aggressiveness, complaining, or living with a perpetual heart posture of disappointment and discontentment. I would later differentiate it as not just being a onetime thing but rather an all-the-time thing. It isn't just a tough season you are working to navigate through; it is the language, behavior, and beliefs that fuel a counterfeit connection in many unhealthy relationships.

Imagine for a moment the last time your mother or sibling called to share some gossip. How did you respond? If common-enemy intimacy is a part of your bonding, you felt drawn to it. Maybe even excited. This excitement is part of why it's so addictive, but it's also why we feel so drained, shallow, and discontent after. It doesn't deliver on what it promises.

If you aren't sure whether your relationships are built on connecting through common-enemy intimacy, start to listen more closely to your conversations. If topics are primarily negative, then this counterfeit connection may be to blame.

How do they typically sound?

What or whom do you talk about?

How is the tone?

Is there judgment? Ridicule? Criticism?

Are you able to connect and interact about anything positive, personal, or progressive?

You may be asking yourself, *What's the big deal? We enjoy venting; it's harmless!* Well, it isn't harmless, actually. Intimacy that is built on negative exchanges is a coping skill that allows you the continued opportunity to avoid your own problems. As I mentioned earlier, distraction is a coping skill. And minimizing this unhealthy behavior is an easy way for you to continue using your focus, energy, and time on others, which in turn distracts you from the areas God wants to work on in you and through your relationships.

It's easy to keep sinning if you can point the finger at everyone else "out there." It's even easier if you have a few people on board, pointing their fingers with you. This helps you feel justified and safe in your little sphere of protection, but it also reinforces the cycle of avoidance. And, friend, God can't shape your heart if you avoid him.

> **Intimacy that is built on negative exchanges is a coping skill that allows you the continued opportunity to avoid your own problems.**

This isn't new behavior, however. We read about it in Scripture, leading up to the crucifixion of Jesus. Pilate sent Jesus to King Herod, and while it is said that both men felt Jesus was innocent, they agreed to his execution; Jesus was then delivered to the "demand" of the crowd.[2] "That day Herod and Pilate became friends—before this they had been enemies" (Luke 23:12).

We learn in Scripture that, through their desire to keep the peace, they sacrificed Jesus, and by uniting against him, *they were no longer enemies.*

So let me ask you—what relationships of yours are built on having a common enemy? In what ways are you repeating patterns of highlighting everyone else's problems, simply because it helps you distract from and tolerate your own?

Perhaps you are just now realizing how influential your childhood environment was and the behaviors that were modeled to you. It can feel like a daunting task to tame something you have been doing, like gossiping with people you love so much, for so long.

Over time it can become a case of the chicken or the egg. Who started this unhealthy connection? And are we striving to manage or cope with the chaos, or are we the ones generating it? Listen, it doesn't matter. This behavior is compulsive and extremely contagious. When one person elicits the behavior, you will generally find many other people stirring the pot too. What you need to take away from this is that a healthy relationship can't survive unhealthy forms of communicating or connecting. Regardless of where it started, it can end with you.

If you grew up in a home where connecting this way was common, it will be helpful to understand the role enmeshment plays. A lot of dysfunctional families are what is considered "enmeshed," which simply means that family members do not have a clear independence from one another. The following are symptoms of an enmeshed family:

- Individuals lack physical and emotional boundaries.
- Parents meddle in personal lives of adult children.
- Parents overshare or depend on children for support.
- Adult children are guilted for pursuing anything that does not include parents.
- Individuals avoid conflict or confrontation.[3]

Enmeshed families have a primary symptom, which is an inability to distinguish one's own feelings, wants, or needs from those of other family members. If you come from an enmeshed family system, you will eventually feel the weight of it. This dynamic can leave you confused or feeling overly responsible for other family members' happiness, health, and well-being.

Boundary setting is the antidote for enmeshed relationships, although limit setting can be felt as a personal attack by some. Disengaging from connecting through any form of common-enemy intimacy may be difficult, but it is not impossible. Some won't like your limits, but you can learn that this isn't yours to manage.

DO BETTER

The fear of facing those you love can be scary and even paralyzing. But, friend, the good news is that you aren't being asked to carry this burden alone. You have a strong, capable, mighty Father who is not confused about your future. He created you in his image, with good, good plans for you. But he needs you to get some of this rubble out of the way. We simply cannot receive his plentiful blessings and allow him to restore our relationships when our hands and hearts are distracted and discouraged. This information can be overwhelming, but I want it to inspire you to act. You don't have to have everything figured out, but you do have to commit that where you are is no longer where you want to stay.

If you are accustomed to connecting with others through negativity and a "common enemy," or if your family culture is doused with language and behavior that consists of complaint, chaos, or manufactured crisis, you can decide today to become intentional about the part you play in these interactions. In the past perhaps you felt powerless, hopeless, and fearful.

But that stops today.

One of the most powerful steps you can take today is simply acknowledging that you have participated to some degree in the denying, justifying, or guarding of dysfunctional behavior in your relationships. Acknowledgment is a powerful conduit to healing. We can't change what we don't first acknowledge.

You may have heard a saying attributed to Maya Angelou that goes something like this: "Do the best you can until you know better. And when you know better, do better." It is time that you do better. No more idly sitting by, passively allowing your relationships to crumble. No more settling for anything less than true, authentic, God-inspired connections.

Looking back on my childhood, I can see clearly how often I rolled with chaos, even going as far as defending it as "normal," simply because these behaviors were persistent enough to convince me that they were. And I had no problem carrying on this behavior, because it was what I knew. Yet after Allison confronted me, I began to exercise self-control and refrain from connecting out of fear and desperation. It wasn't always done perfectly; there were many times I fell victim to the temptation to gossip to feel better about myself. But I knew if I wanted to have healthier relationships, I would have to stop engaging in unhealthy behaviors.

I also realized that honest connection didn't come naturally to me. By criticizing, judging, or gossiping, I was able to hide myself and control the narrative. But in hiding, I couldn't truly connect. I was aiding in my own inability to have meaningful, authentic relationships, and this I had to take full responsibility for.

He gets a thrill out of this, the Enemy. It brings him much pleasure to see all of God's precious relationships fractured. He wants us hiding and disconnected, putting each other down. But we deserve better. Our relationships deserve better. Our neighbors, coworkers, and children deserve better. And those who came before you, who may not have been able to fight the good fight that you are about to embark on, they deserve it too. We can start by worrying less about what others think and start confronting gently, yet honestly, in the same way my friend Allison confronted me.

GET MOVING!

Every year on Thanksgiving morning the community I live in hosts a community 5k called Race for the Pies. And every year since my husband and I were married, we would wake early to participate. It was always a great way to get in some movement on the holiday, and winning a pie never hurt. Now, with four children, this annual ritual looks a bit different. He wakes our older two early to head over for their Pilgrim Dash, a fifty-yard sprint just for the kids to enjoy. After they finish, and just as the big 5k starts, they make their way back on foot to meet the rest of us at the end of our street. Here, neighbors gather with coffees and doughnuts to cheer on the runners passing by.

One year my two-year-old son got a real thrill out of watching the men and women sprint past us, many wearing turkey costumes or pilgrim hats. His little body bobbed up and down as his hands clapped in delight. Shortly after overhearing another onlooker cheer "Winner!" he, too, enthusiastically joined in. His little fist rose high into the sky as he shouted, "Winner! Winner! Winner!" The race wasn't close to being over, but he didn't care. Every runner was a winner in his eyes.

I've got good news, but it may come across as bad news: God isn't going to do all the work for you. In God's eyes you, too, are already a winner. It doesn't matter what place you are in, as long as you stay in the race to finish (Heb. 12:1).

God doesn't need your cooperation, but he wants it. He wants you to take ownership and responsibility. When you are a part of a solution, he knows it is then that you will make lasting change. And lasting change is the key to his glory. Let me share with you a story from the Bible that illustrates this power.

Moses was no stranger to taking action. In Exodus, as Moses was leading the Israelites out of captivity and into freedom, they neared the Red Sea and looked back to see that the pharaoh's army was chasing them down with horses and chariots. Imagine, being so close to freedom and now seeing that opportunity shattered in a matter of minutes.

Afraid, the people cried out to Moses, "Why did you bring us out here to die in the wilderness?" (Ex. 14:11 NLT). It is then that we read about Moses reminding the people that the Lord would rescue them, but it wasn't void of their participation.

> The LORD said to Moses, "Why are you crying out to me? Tell the people to *get moving*! Pick up your staff and raise your hand over the sea. Divide the water so the Israelites can walk through the middle of the sea on dry ground." (Ex. 14:15–16 NLT, emphasis added)

Did you read all the action happening?

Tell the people.

Get moving!

Pick up your staff.

Raise your hand.

Divide the water.

Sometimes we must come face-to-face with our own Red Sea and take action in faith to part its waters. The Lord always hears your cries, friend. He knows the areas that you long for healing in, he knows of the habits and behaviors that are causing you pain, and he knows of the relationships that are unhealthy. Yes, occasionally God will part the water on your behalf, and you will feel immediate freedom and relief. But more times than not, as with Moses, he will give you marching orders and expect you to march. Why? Because he doesn't just want to bestow freedom, healing, and happiness on you—he wants to change you in the process.

Our faith is not passive, and most times it needs a good stirring. Like a fire burning low, your active participation is what will get that fire blazing again. "For this reason I remind you to fan into flame the gift of God, which is in you" (2 Tim. 1:6).

You may be accustomed to hurting, to living a life filled with fear and exhaustion. You may be so used to settling for relationships riddled with distrust, anxiety, and confusion that you can't even imagine anything different. You may, for the very first time now, be acknowledging just how unhealthy some of your close circle is. But God has so much more for you ahead if you would choose to partner with him in the process. If you choose to stir up the fire within, let that flame of faith sustain you.

Keep going and remember—the reward of healthy connection in your relationships is always worth the risk.

GOD'S FORGIVENESS

It is not easy to finish a chapter like this one (especially if you are a self-proclaimed people pleaser or perfectionist) and not feel ashamed or like you failed in some way. I know this because I felt that way before too. We have all played a part in the dysfunction of our former relationships, some more than others. But there is grace for you; this is the beauty of following Christ. Once you ask for God's forgiveness, you receive it immediately. This isn't something you must earn, but it is something you must openly accept. Part of you may feel tempted to live in the condemnation, to continue punishing yourself for the mistakes of your past, or to try to earn your way up some divine ladder, but that is not of God. You are cleansed, so let yourself live as such. Remember, shame does nothing more than continue to hold you in captivity.

———

It wasn't too long ago that my six-year-old daughter and I got into a heated argument. She was upset about something and proceeded to throw a pencil at my face (this is not a joke). Thankfully, I did not lose an eye, but I did lose my temper. Later that night after the dust and emotions settled, we exchanged apologies and accepted each other's forgiveness. The next morning as we were driving to school, she began bickering with her younger sister, and in a weak attempt to control the situation, I brought up the night prior and the pencil-throwing incident.

"Mom," she told me, "the hardest part about that was not you getting hit with the pencil. It was about me hurting God, and that hurt my heart. I asked God to forgive me for that, and then I deleted it out of my brain." (Imagine her little, chubby hand gesturing away from her head, as if pulling something literally from her brain.) Then she went on to say, "And now you bring it baaaack up, and it goes baaaack into my brain . . ." as she pushed her little fingers against her head.

I did everything I could not to laugh.

And she was right.

This is what we do.

We ask for God's forgiveness, and instead of taking it, we allow others and ourselves to push it back into our brains. This all may feel new to you; but you are worthy of this kind of love. Not because you earned it, but because Jesus did.

You are forgiven.

Learn from your mistakes.

Let God use them to shape you.

But don't you dare let them hold you back from what God has in store for you next.

Delete them from your brain.

And let's keep moving.

ACKNOWLEDGE & CONFRONT

1. What unhealthy behaviors are you guarding, minimizing, or defending right now in your relationships?
2. Were you raised in an enmeshed family? Was common-enemy intimacy present?
3. Do you find yourself highlighting other people's problems? How so?
4. What problem of your own right now are you avoiding?
5. Is God asking you to *get moving* like Moses? In what ways can you fan the flame of your faith and partner with him in your relationships?

3

It's All Under Control

IN THE BOOK *DRINKING: A LOVE STORY* BY Caroline Knapp, she wrote that "alcohol has an insidious dual effect of deadening the discomfort and also preventing us from ever really overcoming it; we become too adept at sidestepping the feelings with drink to address them directly."[1]

I didn't know I had an issue with alcohol; I did, however, finally admit to myself that my family did. In fact, generations before me had suffered with addiction in one form or another. I was just really good at convincing myself I had dodged that bullet.

There was no major tipping point that I can recall that sent me over the edge from "social, casual drinker" to "obsessive, compulsive consumer." I do remember when wondering turned into worrying whether alcohol would be served at places I went, and the feeling of relief when it was confirmed that, yes, it would be available. I do remember negotiating with myself about how many I would have, and how many I would not have, and beating myself up when I broke this promise to myself, *again*. I do remember the feelings swirling around inside about how I could never possibly identify with someone who had an addiction problem because I was a straight-A student growing up, an overachiever, and someone who was well-put-together (most of the time). I'd mentally dismiss and debate myself out of owning any part of my inability to control or manage my drinking. The easiest escape from this became blaming others.

I had managed to secure a college scholarship playing a sport I loved dearly—soccer. Yet just before moving away to college, my parents had split and sold our childhood home, which made it difficult to leave. I did attend college for a few semesters, but my mom needed me back home just as much as I wanted to be home, so I dropped out.

I moved back in with my mom and began sharing a room with one of my older brothers, which was as awkward as you would imagine. I remember watching a show one night with him, his bed adjacent to mine, when I asked, "Do you believe in heaven?" It was as if I wanted him to make some sense of the mess we were all now in. I wanted him to point me toward more. Was *this* really all there was for us?

"Shut up, I can't hear the TV," he replied.

And so I did.

We lived in a small two-bedroom house that sat on blocks, in an area of town that was known for drug sales. It was all my mom could afford on her own, and while she did her best to make it nice, it never felt like home. I don't remember feeling scared, I think because most of my life was spent on high alert.

I began bartending at a nearby restaurant while taking courses at the local college. I felt disappointed in myself and angry at my parents. I knew I wasn't responsible for our family falling apart, but I also did not know how to live as if I wasn't. Like I was as a child, I was still tightly tethered to their feelings, wants, and problems. I couldn't solve or fix what was happening around me, but I could numb my emotions, for a while anyway.

Bartending was fun. Since I liked to drink, my job gave me access to alcohol that was always available. Plus, I got to hang out with people who liked to drink too. I liked belonging to a crowd who harbored the same desire to numb like I did. Happy hours were more than just happy; they became my place of refuge. I found solace in both the liquid medicine available and the patrons who came to drink it with me. I would intimately get to know some of these people who bellied up to the bar night after night; after all, I would spend more time with them than with my actual relatives. I would hear about a dying wife or a sick child. I would learn of their business endeavors, what made them laugh, what made them cry. While I knew these people weren't relatives of mine, they gave me something I couldn't find anywhere else. I liked the idea that they were temporary too. Most of them were "snowbirds," enjoying a few warm months in South Florida before heading back north.

As the nights grew darker, happy-hour folks would leave and the serious drinkers would find their way in. By then I'd have had a few myself, so I was ready to up the ante. The music changed to a dance playlist and the candles were lit on the marble bar top. I would slice a few more oranges, shave a few more lemon zests, and skewer another jar full of cocktail olives for the second-round rush. The barback would join me for a quick kamikaze shot in between polishing glassware.

And then it would happen: Something would begin to shift in my body, as if my cells were realigning. I was at just the perfect buzz, with the feeling of warmth inside I had grown to miss. I hit my stride, serving drinks and selling shots. I'd grab a twenty, hollering over the music, "That'll be six fifty!" all while smiling and moving to the next customer. "What can I getcha?" I'd occasionally slide myself up on the bar, wrapping my arms around a friend who came in for a visit. I felt beautiful, powerful—in the spotlight and in control. I would sigh in relief. I'd been waiting for this feeling.

The next morning I would wake around 10:00 a.m. with a raging headache, just as I had done every other morning after a shift bartending. If I was fortunate, I would wake up alone. The sun would hurt my face, so I avoided it.

I need water. I need to brush my teeth. God, I did it again. I hate myself.

The day would be spent trying to get something into my belly to fuel my body to do some sort of movement. Maybe laundry, but usually just lying around. My thoughts would inflict so much more pain: *You are an idiot. How could you do this? When will you ever learn? Let's stick to only two tonight, no shots, only wine, got it?*

I'd look at the clock. I needed to get ready.

It took all the energy I had to get into the shower. Brushing my hair hurt. I had the runs. *Am I dying?*

Makeup wouldn't help. I looked tired; I looked empty. I felt tired; I felt empty.

I'd throw on my wrinkled, sometimes still-dirty uniform and walk out the door. And the insanity of the night prior would repeat, again and again.

This cycle went on for many years. I was making a lot of cash, so leaving to get a day job that didn't offer very much compensation and had zero access to alcohol didn't make sense. I had fun bartending and drinking; that is, until I didn't. But I believed deep in my soul that I could control the amount I had, that I could change who I was, that I could make myself different whenever I wanted to. I couldn't come to terms with just how deep the Enemy's claws were in me. I didn't want to face the truth that I wasn't very different from my own family after all.

This drinking of mine did not come across as problematic to anyone else. Alcohol was part of my relationships and the culture I was raised in. It was what we did together. When we grieved, we drank. When we celebrated, we drank. When we were bored, or traveling, or doing housework, we drank. Every direction I looked, someone, somehow, struggled with chasing something outside themselves to feel better, and these strongholds wanted nothing more than to kill and destroy us (John 10:10).

MARRIAGE

Jim was someone who, after we first met, I felt I had known my whole life. I was twenty-five and still bartending when we were introduced through some mutual friends. I was instantly drawn to him and not sure why. Was it his wit? Maturity? Self-assurance? Maybe it was his stability and confidence, both of which I lacked. I had asked him to dinner (more than once), but he was seeing someone else. Until one day he called to say he was finally single, and a relationship quickly blossomed.

I would like to write that our walk to the altar was seamless, but it was far from living out a fairy tale. Baggage like mine doesn't suddenly disappear just because you fall in love.

He proposed on his birthday, at sunrise on a beach in the Dominican Republic, and I did what I hear most women do once they are newly engaged: I started planning our wedding. The following summer we exchanged vows, yet once the excitement of the wedding was over, I was left to do what I didn't know how to do: *be married*. I quickly realized that this union didn't fix or fulfill me as I had hoped it would.

I finally had the stability I longed for. I was no longer bartending and had a safe place to call home, a car that didn't break down, and the marriage I had always prayed for. Yet I didn't feel complete. I still ached. I still felt unworthy and alone. Wasn't he *the one*? And, if so, why didn't I feel better?

It didn't take me very long to start arguments that didn't need to happen. I barked at him about the silliest things, casting bait his way hoping for a bite. More times than not he rose above my shallow attempts at conflict, yet on occasion he would be pushed too far, and yelling would ensue. I look back now after all these years and can see that this pattern of behavior was repeated from childhood. I didn't know how to engage in healthy disagreements. In fact, I didn't know how to *be* in a healthy relationship. A relationship void of chaos and unpredictability felt odd, uncomfortable, and, at times, even boring.

I wasn't happy, and neither was he. I didn't have my old roles to play, like caretaker or fixer or therapist, as my husband was already on solid ground. What he needed was a wife, and a sober one. And while I thought leaving the bartending gig would help my drinking, it didn't. We were just five months married and my consumption had hit an all-time high. I didn't know how to deal with the emptiness, so I did what I knew how to do best.

I avoided, lied, hid, and numbed.

One morning in early October of 2014, I called in sick again for work. I was a Pilates instructor at a nearby gym and let my clients know I wasn't feeling well. I had overdone it the night before with some girlfriends and was in no shape to instruct a class.

My husband kissed me goodbye as I stood in my pajamas. He had some work meetings to attend, and little did he know I had plans of my own. After he closed the front door, I walked to the kitchen cabinet, grabbed a white coffee mug, and filled it with whiskey. It wasn't my preference, but I had already worked my way through the champagne and wine.

I walked back up to our bedroom, pulled the blinds shut, and climbed into bed, turning on *Kathie Lee & Hoda*. They drank most mornings, too, so I didn't feel so bad about it.

Suddenly, in he walked. He had forgotten something, only to return home to find me at my absolute lowest moment.

What happened after that is nothing short of a miracle and testimony of God's grace. My husband called a friend, who was connected with a local rehab center. I was terrified, but I knew if I didn't pack my bags and go, I never would. The next day I entered a thirty-day treatment program and have been sober ever since.

UNSPOKEN AGREEMENTS

Have you ever found yourself a part of something and asked, "Wait, did I agree to this?" That's exactly what this moment was like. For the first time I began looking at my life from a different perspective. It's as if I had been simply agreeing to things without my own awareness up until that point, and suddenly I was waking up from a bad dream.

I had been on the hunt for over a decade, trying to calm the confusion inside, trying to bandage up the insecurities, trying to silence the shame of my childhood, trying to find something or someone to make it all better. Yet by binding myself to anything or anyone that promised me temporary security and peace, I had drifted far from God. It was in those moments of desperation and solitude, at my darkest, that I finally understood he could and would do more with my surrender than with my control.

Maybe for you it's not about struggles with a drink or drug. But I can guarantee if you look hard enough, there is a lineage of sin that has some of your family members in bondage, threatening to take you down with it.

Maybe it is the way women in your family use, see, and speak about their bodies. Maybe it is a struggle with overworking or over-achieving. Maybe it is a destructive relationship with food, vanity, or money. Maybe it is generations of infidelity, sex addiction, or divorce. Maybe there are hidden issues with anger and resentment or some other form of spiritual idolatry or stronghold that is wreaking havoc on your heart. Whatever it is, it's a desire to control and claim for oneself a quick fix, a shallow and temporary remedy, a reprieve from discomfort.

How tragic it is when we choose to chase something or someone in pursuit of a remedy, without admit-ting that by doing so we are taking steps away from the very remedy we need.

Sometimes I joke to my husband that he saved me. We both know that isn't true. He did, however, tell me "no more" when I needed it the most. This is when I first experi-enced the true meaning of love and loyalty—drawing a line when it is hard. I thought getting sober would be the hardest thing I ever had to do. I was wrong. Learning how to be in relationship with family mem-bers who were living a different way would be.

> **How tragic it is when we choose to chase something or someone in pursuit of a remedy, without admitting that by doing so we are taking steps away from the very remedy we need.**

ACKNOWLEDGE & CONFRONT

1. Do you ever find yourself blaming someone or something for your inability to pursue change? What does this look like?

2. In what way have you chased security, peace, or love in the wrong outlets?

3. Have you agreed to unspoken rules or unhealthy behaviors in your close relationships? How is this drawing you away from God?

4. Does stability or consistency ever feel boring to you?

5. Has anyone told you no out of authentic love and loyalty? How did you respond?

4

Honoring Those Before You

YOU MAY BE ASKING, HOW CAN I BREAK FREE from what is holding me back without destroying my relationships? Especially if those I care about most don't want to change?

I think it is safe to say that many women fear whistleblowing on the sin they witness because they fear angering, upsetting, or losing a connection with people they love the most. More so, many wounded families who claim to be Christian can in fact use the very gospel against one another.

Say you grew up with a relatively "normal" childhood. Your parents worked hard, and you felt you always had what you needed. But as you got older, you began noticing some patterns of behavior that you didn't really see before. Your parents argued, and your dad would disappear for a few days. Your mother would shut down, perhaps being short-tempered with you. You also noticed that your mother kept you and the house exceptionally tidy. You weren't allowed to be in public unless every hair on your head was combed and your dress was stain- and wrinkle-free. You always felt she cared more about the way you looked than how you felt or thought. You never could relax and play like the other kids, and you certainly never felt you could question her or the confusion because you somehow knew you had to cater to her needs.

Now you are married and a mother yourself. You find it especially challenging to face conflict within your marriage. You, too, have the urge to be short with your husband and children. You become passive-aggressive and belittling, unable to address confrontation in a healthy way. You even struggle with how your baby looks in public, and this pains you, because it reminds you of the pressure you felt as a child.

You know you are repeating a cycle that leaves you feeling ashamed, yet you don't know how to break free. You constantly berate yourself and your body, comparing and competing with other women in your life—never feeling enough as a wife or a mother or a friend, and this grieves you because you know you are actively passing this unhealed mess on to your own relationships. If that wasn't enough, you feel angry and resentful of your parents. Most of the time you spend together, you feel triggered, irritated, and annoyed. You think to yourself, *If they would have handled their own baggage, I wouldn't have had to as a child, and none of this would be happening to me now. It's unfair.*

This is all becoming more obvious to you, yet you feel stuck and unable to talk about it openly. Why? Because you have been led to believe that confronting the dysfunction and unhealthy patterns would be dishonoring to your family. Perhaps because you have been on the receiving end of hearing this: "Honor your father and mother" (Eph. 6:2).

So instead of pursuing the best of what God has next for you, you absorb and carry the weight of everyone's discomfort, pain, and confusion, telling yourself how normal your childhood was and that *you should feel grateful that it wasn't worse.*

Sound familiar?

Now, maybe your parents weren't as involved as you had needed them to be. Maybe you had another relative or friend as your primary caregiver. But the underlying limiting belief is still the same, and so are the consequences of falling for this manipulation.

This scripture was never intended to harm you. Yet it can extinguish a woman's ability to mother her child differently than the way she was mothered. It is the scripture that keeps a daughter's lips sealed and free from boldly identifying and rebuking sin. It is the scripture that suffocates a sister from communicating the honest and necessary limits that she craves and deserves. It is the scripture that is stuck on repeat in the minds of Christian women everywhere, exasperating and falsely confirming the fears and anxieties that she knows all too well, the ones that incessantly remind her that she must honor those who came before her even if it means abandoning herself.

HONOR VERSUS OBEDIENCE

It is interesting that in many Christian households children are told to honor their father and mother, yet no one spends much time considering what this *really means*. I think many people (me included) are confused into believing that honoring your parents means to obey them. Children are asked to be obedient as part of God's design to ensure they receive both provision and protection from their parents, presuming that parents themselves are first being obedient to God. Parents are responsible for shaping a child's character and molding her heart to be more like his, and this hierarchy of sorts aids in that process. Unfortunately, this isn't always the case.

As you mature into an independent adult, how you honor your parents will look different from how it did when you were a child, as you are no longer asked by God to remain obedient to them.

Honor may mean

- respecting your parents by disengaging from a conversation before you say something you don't mean;
- praying for them at a distance;
- refraining from engaging in the family drama;
- practicing self-control, allowing them to handle their own problems; or
- living out the calling God has placed on your life even if they don't agree.

When I entered sobriety, I didn't know how to be in relationship with my family anymore. I only knew that the old way of doing things wouldn't work. It wasn't my intention to hurt them, but that's what happened anyway, and it's what often happens when people take steps toward healing.

The first gathering I attended sober was my older brother's wedding reception. He had recently tied the knot and planned a small celebration with close friends and family at his home. I showed up a bit late, just after noon, to find most of the guests already wasted. Shots were being handed out on the pool deck, while my parents and cousins stood around with drinks in hand chitchatting.

I immediately knew I didn't belong there.

For the first time I realized that spending time with people I loved could potentially derail my healing progress.

I had to choose.

My mom later told me that I wasn't as fun as I used to be when I was drinking. It hurt, partly because I knew she was right, and partly because I longed for things to be the way they used to be, even though I knew they couldn't be anymore. It took me a while to learn that I was becoming a different kind of fun, and that fun wasn't for everyone.

I left my brother's house that day on a bad note. The alcohol and feelings had a head-on collision, just as they had on many other afternoons. My father said some hurtful things to me and my new husband, words that I have since worked very hard to forget but haven't. I know now that he was hurting too. I sobbed the entire drive home.

What they didn't know that day was that I had just found out I was pregnant with my first child. Not only was I newly sober, but I was beginning to dream what my new little family would be like. And while it felt like removing drugs and alcohol from the equation was a good start, I now understood that removing unhealthy patterns of being in relationship with each other would have to soon follow.

Two years passed before I saw my parents again, and to this day my brothers have yet to meet any of my four children. This was not an easy season, as when you become a mother to your first child, you want nothing more than for your own mother to be there. You want to ask her how to swaddle your new infant, you want to talk to her about the long, sleepless nights, you want to feel supported, loved, and held too.

But I had to decide that I would honor my parents without remaining obedient to them and their ways, instead choosing to remain obedient to God alone. I had to set my eyes on eternity and the legacy I wanted to one day leave behind. And I knew dreaming about my new family wouldn't be enough; I would have to put in the work to build and intentionally guard it. The journey has been a privilege, although at times painful, reaping me both immense heartache and joy.

WHAT IS HONOR, REALLY?

Honoring those before you, those you love the most, doesn't mean putting yourself in unhealthy environments or circumstances. It doesn't mean involving yourself in gatherings, conversations, or assignments that hold you down or back.

In fact, honoring those who came before you often means choosing to set and maintain healthy, loving boundaries. What our society has come to perpetuate is a message that pressures adult women to stay tightly tethered to their unhealed parents because "they are family." And while we think this pressure will somehow foster community, fellowship, and life's greatest moments together, we instead see dysfunctional patterns that are inherited and passed down through the generations. We must open our perspective; many unhealed parents will beg their children to honor them, when this is simply an attempt to control their now adult child.

You are not dishonoring your family name because you are boldly taking steps to pursue God and the restoration and healing he has promised you. You are not dishonoring your family because you are choosing to no longer pretend or lie about toxic, chaotic, or unhealthy behaviors. Part of surrendering is reminding yourself repeatedly that your walk with God doesn't dishonor them. Sin is, and has always been, to blame.

> **Part of surrendering is reminding yourself repeatedly that your walk with God doesn't dishonor them.**

We know that the primary place where a child is to be taught about faith is the home. In the Bible, God teaches caregivers to train up a child in the way they should go (Prov. 22:6). What happens, then, if parents are not training up their child in the way Scripture describes? What if we experience firsthand parents choosing corruption, sin, and priorities of their own will over God's? What then?

It would be a disservice for me to

tell you what to do when challenging your own family system. It is impossible and irresponsible for me to attempt to write some detailed prescription specific for you.

But I know who can.

I can't give you the words to pray or what first steps to take to break the chains holding you and others you love captive.

But I know who can.

I may not have the answers or even the comfort you need right now reading this, but I can share with you what has helped me take those first steps toward healing.

It had been years since I had stepped foot inside a church. But as I drew close to God and worked to surrender—my addiction, my family, the expectations, my disappointments and dissatisfaction, all the mistakes, shortcomings, all the confusion and hurt—I slowly began to understand who I was in Christ. I started reading my Bible again, and just as the Word says to, I asked God questions. I sought out his comfort and answers. And I began to receive and live out fully the identity he has for me (Matt. 7:7–8).

Walking in a manner worthy of the gospel was not always easy. Sometimes it meant going against what my parents, siblings, and extended family needed or wanted. This meant not accepting invitations to attend certain gatherings that would derail my sobriety and well-being. Often it meant declining a call or ignoring a text. At the very least, it meant no longer allowing my heart and mind to be consumed by their behavior or choices.

I quit being tolerant to sin and started loving the sinners in my life according to how God asks me to, not how the world does. I learned how to separate what they did from who they are and accepted that their unhealthy choices don't have to become mine. I started honoring my family without honoring, denying, or hiding their wounds—using healthy boundaries to guard myself from repeating toxic cycles. I was finally allowing myself to pursue a life different from theirs, without shame or guilt.

Let me remind you, nowhere in the Bible does it say to be tolerant of painful, toxic, or unhealthy relationships. Nowhere does it ask you to be passive to dysfunctional behavior. It does share of your eternal destiny and provides insight into the riches and glory we will get to receive as heirs to the kingdom through faith. It does provide you promises and solace during your times of confusion and insecurity. And more than anything else, it gives us all the gift of knowing who we really belong to in eternity, because sometimes who we belong to here isn't enough. Let God provide you with that, friend. I know he can if you let him.

A DIVINE PARENT

Take comfort in this: "Though my father and mother forsake me, the LORD will receive me" (Ps. 27:10).

I don't know what the future holds for you and your family. You may be disconnected from them, unable to receive the closure you need. You may be facing a season of uncertainty, overwhelmed by the heaviness and pain that sin is causing. You may feel isolated and alone, the only one even considering ways in which you can break free from these strongholds for good. You may be a mother working your hardest to break cycles of dysfunction, and that at times can feel like holding back a tidal wave to protect your children. I do trust that if you go to God for guidance, comfort, and strength, he will give it to you. "So do not fear, for I am with you; do not be dismayed, for I am your God. I will strengthen you and help you; I will uphold you with my righteous right hand" (Isa. 41:10).

When I began to rebuke the sin in my family and separate myself, a mentor of mine encouraged me with something I hope brings peace to you. She reminded me that whatever we didn't get here from our earthly family will be overflowing for us completely in heaven. The affection, approval, and love you craved in this place will be found waiting for you in eternity.

Every heartache, disappointment, and painful moment will be covered by his love and grace when he receives you in heaven. But he doesn't want you to just wait until then, because he has freedom and healing available for you now. The loneliness, uncertainty, and feelings of being less than, lost, or left out will slowly dissipate when you run straight toward God. Place every fear, hurt, and question you have on the altar. I promise you, he has been waiting for you and can handle whatever baggage you have, and more.

A GOOD GOD

No single person was raised in a perfect home. None of us received perfectly secure attachment with our caregivers. All of us have experienced some form of trauma, no matter how big or small. Even the most well-meaning parents fall short. We all have things in our past that have left us feeling unsafe, unloved, and insecure. Why? Because we are being raised in a fallen world, by flawed humans. This is our reality.

It is no wonder our armor is thick. Our coping skills on point. Our numbing and performing an easy go-to. We don't know how to deal with the pain, confusion, and disappointment. It can be daunting to read that your first formative relationships caused more than just pain in childhood, that they may be in part responsible for why you have been believing and behaving in ways that are not you.

Unworthy.

Unloved.

Forgotten.

When we are hurt by those closest to us, it is easy to believe that no one has our best interests at heart. It is easy to keep on living independent, hardened, and detached. After all, it feels safer. It ensures that no one can ever get close enough to hurt you again.

Even God.

When those who were meant to love, protect, and cherish you fell short, how can you believe that this is God's will for you? When you needed acceptance, approval, and affection as a child and didn't get it, how can you believe that God accepts, approves, and loves you now? When the very people who were meant to protect you in fact harmed you, how can you find refuge and solace in the one who is greater?

When we feel these ways, we withdraw from God. We take our hurts, disappointments, and anger out on him instead of giving it all to him. We begin to believe that God is who we *feel* he is instead of who he says he is.

But can I tell you something? He isn't afraid of your anger. He isn't overwhelmed by your hurt. He isn't surprised by your questions. He isn't confused by your confusion. And no matter how bad you may have had it, you still have access to a good God.

ACKNOWLEDGE & CONFRONT

1. What have you been taught to believe about "honoring" those before you? How does this "honoring" hold you back from setting healthy boundaries?
2. What did this chapter teach you about the difference between honoring others and remaining obedient to them?
3. Do you find yourself remaining tolerant of painful, toxic, or unhealthy relationships simply because they are with a family member or a close friend?
4. Have you ever felt guilty about pursuing healing or change? Why?
5. Complete the family tree below to identify where within your lineage (or close friendships) sin may be active and present. Examples include envy, doubt, perfectionism, lying, bitterness, anger, anxiety, manipulation, drunkenness, greed, lust, idolatry, adultery, hatred, distrust, workaholism, and so on.

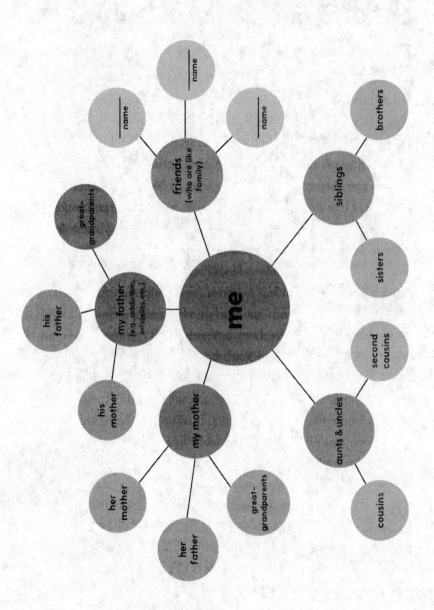

5

What Does Healing Look Like?

GOD HEALS, BUT THAT HEALING MAY NOT MEET our expectations.

I don't know about you, but I have been led astray before. I have had people in my life who I admired, people who I felt had my very best intentions at heart, let me down. I have had people who were meant to care for me inflict pain upon me. I have trusted in others, later to find out that who they were was all a lie. And I believed God would mend all this. I wanted to know that he would help me through. And while he always did, the plan he had for my healing didn't always match up with the plan *I* had for my healing.

We all tend to want instant relief, which is why it is common to cling to things or people that bring it to us when we want it most, only to find out that this sort of relief doesn't last. Here we can begin to live distracted by our own disappointments and discouragements. We may even grow angry at God for not coming through in the way we wanted and needed him to, at a time when it was most convenient for us. It's understandable to want to know when the discomfort will stop so we can move on with our lives.

But guess what happens when we do this? We add to our own suffering. By hanging on to the standards of what we think our healing and blessing should look like, we throw away the healing and blessing available to us now. We sit idle, wondering why God hasn't done what he promises. We wait for these expectations to be fulfilled and miss out on everything he has for us and is asking of us. We want healing from God before we will go to work for God. I was no exception.

COPING

My new therapist was helping me see, for the first time ever, just how powerfully my earliest childhood relationships affected my adult ones. I felt as though I had a clean slate, which was exciting yet overwhelming. I didn't know how to be in relationship with other people without relying on the old patterns of behavior or roles.

As I mentioned earlier, the most common roles I had always played were some form of people-pleasing, performing, or pretending. Inside these roles I could manufacture a sense of safety through control. In most cases I would find myself doing something for others that they weren't yet willing to do for themselves. This is how I would keep their love and earn a spot in their life. It is also how I was loving them well. Or so I thought.

When my therapist and I began to unpack why I repeatedly did this, we noticed a pattern. I had always sought out relationships that needed me in this same way. I had a longing and an attraction to others who couldn't care for, tend to, or handle their own problems. I realized it was because I didn't feel worthy of healthy, safe, reciprocal relationships. It was also why I would often feel used, resentful, and disappointed.

Maybe for you, you received the message that you weren't enough as you are. And over time you began creating a more presentable version of yourself—the go-with-the-flow (but deeply hurting inside) type, the "yes" friend (who is already overwhelmed and exhausted), or the one who can put out all the fires and clean up all the messes (just not her own).

This version you created was well received, which only reinforced this kind of coping. Everybody liked and needed you, *yay!* And since you didn't like who you were anyway, doing all these other things made you feel pretty darn good about yourself. But over time you began to carry more than your part, and this lifting grew costly. So much that now you don't even know who you are or what is yours to carry.

Life now is consumed by catering to the wants, needs, thoughts, expectations, and feelings of others. Your anchor and identity are found in the relationships that need you. It feels scary to imagine not being what you have always been for other people. Will they accept and love you if you suddenly stop?

Change can feel daunting. I know for me, when I first began to unpack who I was without being who others needed me to be, I couldn't even decide on a place to eat lunch. This is what coping through codependency does; it paralyzes. I was so accustomed to caring for everyone else that I didn't know how to care for myself.

And then I was presented with a choice. I could accept the pain of staying the same or choose to endure the pain of change.

PICK YOUR PAIN

I knew how to live in pain. Staying the same was comfortable, predictable, even easy. I knew all about migraines, panic attacks, insomnia, digestion issues, and cold sores. I knew all about blaming others for my suffering and never having to own up to my stuff. I knew how to live bitter, angry, hurt, and betrayed. It was familiar pain, but I was getting tired of it. I was getting tired of me.

I learned I had another option. I could lean into the pain of change. That would mean letting go of all the old coping skills and unhealthy patterns of behavior that had served me for so long. For the first time I had to choose discomfort and not run from it. I had to feel all the feelings and think all the thoughts. I had to get real and honest with myself. I had to put on my big-girl pants. I had to take responsibility. I had to ask God for help.

I had to pick my pain.

If I was going to be in pain, I at least wanted to get something out of it. But this new pain of choosing change came with an unexpected element: I had to get good at allowing those I love to feel their own pain too. Sitting in the discomfort of that at times felt unbearable. I could be hurting, but witnessing others in their pain without jumping to their rescue? Ughhh.

You see, we all find ways to cope with discomfort. We absorb and consume the upset and confusion of everyone because it helps us feel needed, helpful, and, in a lot of ways, busy. Yet it is how we stay in bondage to ourselves.

Recently a writer I admire shared a newsletter in which she touched on this very subject. She wrote that her remedy for people-pleasing and working so hard to get others to love her was by fighting for these people to love God instead.[1]

Aha moment, right?

Maybe that's why God put so much desire in us to love others well, and perhaps this is why so many of us fall short. Serving them was never meant for our benefit *but for his.* When you make this paradigm shift, not only does it bless those around you with a gift you couldn't ever produce yourself, but it also breaks you free from using your old coping tendencies. You quit worshiping their approval and begin to worship him instead. You let go of living a life others expect you to live and commit to the higher calling of kingdom work. When you stay clear on whom you are serving, you no longer fear their disappointment, because you know pointing them back to him is always worth this cost.

I once heard a song that said, "If it's not good yet, then God's not done yet." We have a good God, even if the pain of our past isn't very good. Yes, sometimes there are long, painful seasons of waiting. Lots of discomfort. It takes trust—trusting God for the plans he has for you and letting go of the plans you have for you. It takes faith—faith that is fanned through acting obediently despite the discomfort. And it takes "settling in," pledging to do the work he is asking you to do, right where you are—even when you don't feel like doing it. We can believe that if it isn't good yet, then he isn't done yet.[2]

Remember, God can see what his children can't. His views are wide; his love is deep (Eph. 3:18). He sees ultimate freedom and healing, not just for us but for our relationships, for our families, for our children, for our communities.

Wow. I want all of that. But it won't just fall into my lap. And it most likely won't fall into yours either.

I can decide to believe God has a good plan for me even if I can't see it yet.

I can decide to trust that he will handle those who harmed me.

I can decide to call on him, pray to him, seek him, and find him.

I can decide to go to work for him as I wait on my ultimate healing.

I can decide to live with gratitude because his mercy shines on me.

I can decide to look at where I have been, not to stay there but to choose not to return there. I can learn from the patterns of dysfunction that fell before me and begin to walk a different path. My hope is that this next section is going to help you get started.

FAMILY OF ORIGIN INVENTORY

I truly believe healing and freedom are possible, or I wouldn't have written this book. I have a firm hope that when we acknowledge the patterns of behavior that are unhealthy in our relationships, and those relationships that came before us, we can begin to break free from them and leave a legacy we are proud of.

Healthy relationships can directly impact and change the world. At times it may feel as though you are facing an uphill battle, especially if generations before you were held captive by strongholds and lies of the Enemy.

In fact, it may feel impossible to even imagine yourself inside healthy relationships. I get it because I was once there too. You may be staring at what looks like a large pile of debris, unsure of where to even begin.

Much of what we're going to explore together about your family of origin isn't just for awareness purposes. You will have to take necessary steps to set down old inherited patterns of believing, thinking, and acting to make room for new patterns. This will take intention and a personal commitment from you. It will require loads of patience and grace. At times you will grow weary. You may even begin to wonder if what you are doing now to change even matters. You may long to return to old people, places, or patterns of behavior that once brought you solace and comfort. But if you can stay the course, the reward is grand.

Like a ripple effect when a stone is cast into a pond, what you are doing now is affecting far more than you can comprehend. There is no telling the lives you are changing by what you are choosing to face head-on today. It is my prayer that generations after you will one day be thanking you for the work you are doing now.

Coping through playing an unhealthy role is simply a means to an end. You learned to do so for any number of reasons, one of which may be because you felt you didn't have any other choice. The truth is that we are always making choices, whether we realize it or not. Right now you are making a choice to pursue wholeness. I hope you continue to choose this, especially when it is hard, and even when others don't like it.

So what does a healthy family system even look like?

Here are some characteristics:

- healthy autonomy modeled by caregivers
- mutual respect, affection, and appreciation
- ability to manage crises and conflicts
- safety to be seen, heard, and known
- boundaries modeled and encouraged
- clear expectations and core values
- shared sense of humor and joy together
- predictable and consistent routines
- space for making mistakes and receiving grace
- honest and open communication[3]

No caregiver or family is perfect, and therefore not every childhood was a good one. Consider the following exercise like collecting data. Remember, it isn't about pointing fingers or casting blame. What you do with this data will be up to you. Who you are today can no longer be shaped by an old or default coping skill. You can bring forward all that matters and leave in the past all that doesn't.

Taking a family of origin (FOO) inventory will help you better understand the context in which you developed a sense of self. We inherit scripts, beliefs, and behaviors (both positive and negative) about ourselves and others from our family of origin. This early conditioning can influence who you are today and the way in which you show up for yourself and for your relationships. My hope is that this information is used as fuel for lasting change.

For example, Danielle—a woman in my online coaching community, Discover Your Worth (DYW)—has parents who got a divorce when she was in middle school. At first she didn't believe this had too much of an impact on her adult relationships. But once she did the FOO inventory, she realized that the way her mother spoke to and about her father (in disrespectful and belittling tones) is also how she tends to speak to her own husband now when under stress. She also noticed a strong correlation with the way she disciplines her children and the way her parents disciplined her. She remembered that after her parents' divorce she encountered a lot of inconsistent routines and unclear expectations between homes, which made discipline both confusing and unpredictable. With this newfound knowledge she was better able to decide for herself how she wanted to be both as a wife and a mother, as opposed to falling back on her old conditioning by default.

> **When you become aware of the framework that has shaped your past, you can take responsibility for shaping your future.**

It is important to keep in mind that birth order can alter one's view on family of origin, which may be why your inventory could be different from a sibling's. You can also expect your perception to change as you gain new insight into past interactions. Because of this, it is not a bad idea to return to your FOO inventory later for review and reassessment. Again, this is a tool to spark your curiosity, hopefully providing you with some insight that ultimately inspires lasting change.

When you become aware of the

framework that has shaped your past, you can take responsibility for shaping your future. This involves making intentional choices about what behaviors will come with you and what will be left behind.

Before starting, begin in prayer. Ask God to reveal to you the areas that may be directly affecting your life now. Ask him to provide you with strength, clarity, and wisdom. Don't condemn or judge what comes up for you; lean into the grace available for you today. Remember, this is powerful data that can help you establish new behaviors in your relationships that you can be proud of. If at any time you feel overwhelmed or discouraged, take a break. There is no rush.

You may find that some of the unhealthy behaviors you engage in today are in part due to the effects of early conditioning and the behaviors that were first modeled to you. My hope is that throughout the rest of this book, you will find practical tools to help unlearn some of these behaviors and replace them with healthier, God-honoring behaviors instead.

Note: This inventory is not intended to be a substitute for professional advice, diagnosis, medical treatment, medication, or therapy. Always seek the advice of your physician or qualified Christian certified mental health provider with any questions you may have regarding any mental health symptoms or medical condition. I am not authorized to make recommendations about medication or to provide materials that serve as a substitute for professional advice. Never disregard professional psychological care or delay in seeking professional advice or treatment because of something you have read.

FOO INVENTORY

ASK:	COMMUNICATION	AFFECTION	SAFETY	VALUES	DISCIPLINE	FAITH	HEALTH
	What styles of speaking were modeled? ·Passive ·Aggressive ·Both	Was affection withheld or consistent?	Did you feel safe mentally, emotionally, and physically with them?	What does this person value?	Was discipline clear and predictable? If not, what was it like?	What was modeled to you about God, faith, or a higher power?	What was the state or their mental, physical, and emotional health?
MOM							
DAD							
SIBLING							
AUNT							
COACH							
OTHER CAREGIVER							

MY NOTES

_____

_____

_____

_____

_____

_____

_____

_____

_____

_____

_____

_____

_____

_____

_____

_____

_____

ACKNOWLEDGE & CONFRONT

1. Have you ever been upset with God because his healing for you (or your relationships) didn't meet your expectations? Explain.
2. What is your favorite way to cope when you encounter discomfort (shopping, social media, drinking, gossip, sleep, etc.)?
3. Is there a person you are working hard to please? What would happen if you put that energy into helping them love God instead of you?
4. How are you at witnessing or allowing others you care about experience their own pain? Do you tend to jump to their rescue or insert yourself with solutions/help? Describe a recent example.
5. Take some time to work through the FOO inventory and use the extra notes section for further processing. Consider the points below as you do.

   • Consider both positive and negative memories. Describe the times when you were happy and the times you were sad, scared, or confused.
   • What feelings can you remember craving more of (like safety or affection)?
   • What were you grateful for as a child?
   • Did you have to care for a caregiver or sibling? If so, how?
   • Do you have a favorite memory? A least favorite memory?
   • In what ways do you believe your life would be different if you had different parents/caregivers? Describe what these different caregivers would be like (qualities, gifts, behaviors, beliefs, etc.).

6

Codependency

CODEPENDENCY IS A TERM I FIRST LEARNED IN AN Adult Children of Alcoholics (ACA) meeting. Learning about codependency helped me understand how I had contributed to losing myself in my relationships. I began reading the book *Codependent No More* by Melody Beattie, and it changed the way I viewed boundaries forever. You know the way your eyes slowly adjust when you walk into a dark room, and you begin to see? It was like that.

I started working with a group of ACA women; we would meet for meetings and mingle over coffee afterward. While some of my old "party" girlfriends had slowly faded away, I still had some close friends that remained. One friend in particular, Ashley, meant a whole lot to me as we had a ton of shared history. We would text daily and chat about everything. We borrowed each other's clothes, went to the salon for pedicures, and tried to meet once a week or more for lunch. She felt more like a sister than a friend.

But things slowly started changing between her and me. At first I couldn't pinpoint what the shift was. Then I realized: *it was me*. I was changing.

The relationship we once had no longer served who I was or where I was headed. I didn't find it necessary to chat as much as we always did. I went back to school, started writing for the newspaper, and even began playing pickleball. In fact, the constant stream of texts between us started to feel suffocating. Then I noticed how irritated I would become after we spent time together, as I realized her lack of boundary setting compared to mine.

One afternoon I met up with Ashley for an acai bowl. Within minutes, it seemed, she began to share details about her recent health scare. "I am overdoing it," she said, "burning the candle at both ends."

She went on to tell me that her doctor ran her blood panels, and her cortisol levels were through the roof. "I am not sleeping well, and I almost passed out on a run the other morning. I think it's because I didn't eat."

The solutions I gave her seemed obvious to me. "Why don't you try resting? Take some time off from the gym, quit overcommitting yourself. And, for goodness' sake, eat a solid meal."

"On it, I promise!" she replied.

But then it happened again. The dizzy episodes. The migraines. The overexerting herself past her limit. And of course she'd tell me *all* about it. And the irritating cycle would start again.

It was then that I realized my *concern* for her had turned into being *consumed* by her. Playtime with my kids would be derailed by thoughts of *I wonder if she overdid it today again* . . . Date night with my husband would include conversations about her, as if she were our third wheel. And I began sharing my concern (ahem, *control*) with other mutual friends, which was really just gossip, something I swore to myself I would quit.

My care had crossed a line, and I knew this for certain because the connection and ease I once felt with her turned into sour criticism and contempt. My pride had taken over, and so had my old role of unhelpful helping, aka *codependency*.

I shared with a friend in ACA about the dilemma I was up against. She had been in the program for much longer than I, so I knew she would have wise counsel. "I care about her, but I am beginning to see just how codependent our relationship is. I told myself for a while I was just being a good friend, but I think staying connected to her is serving me in some unhealthy way . . ."

"You can't control her outcome, you know. You can't control how or if or when she will take care of herself. What you *can* control is how far you let yourself go down that old codependent path," she said.

That is what codependency is. You take on others' problems as if they are your own. You become highly focused on their feelings, activities, and choices. Over time your well-being becomes dependent on their well-being, and to some degree you even feel responsible for it.

She went on to say, "Eventually you will have to accept that boundaries will be how you can safely manage to stay in relationship with her. But the first boundary you must place *is the one on yourself.*"

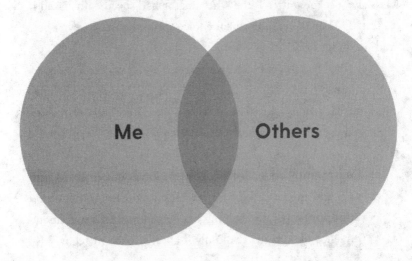

HEALTHY OVERLAP

Me

Others

All my caretaking in the past, as much as I hated to admit it, was actually hurting those I cared about. And while at times it provided some temporary relief from the problem, it only perpetuated the cycle of victimization for us both. It also prevented a major component necessary for change. As Melody Beattie writes, "We jam ourselves between people and God. We make it easy for people to avoid taking *responsibility* for themselves"[1] (emphasis added).

If I were going to be different in our relationship, I would have to start doing things differently. This first started by quite literally sitting on my hands. When Ashley sent a text, I began to respond with less urgency. I would let hours, sometimes days, pass before typing out an answer. I knew this would be a crucial step and one I would have to be consistent with in becoming less consumed by her. Funny thing happened too—I found the less we talked, the more connected to her I felt. The intentional space allowed me to breathe and appreciate her more.

I also silenced all her social media updates. I get how silly and immature this all sounds. But it made a huge difference in our relationship. Why? Because I would no longer see her updates about a spin class she just took after I knew her doctor had specifically asked her to rest. This small yet intentional choice allowed me to love her better and not judge her.

Finally, I had to get honest with myself about why this codependent relationship was still serving me, after all the work I had done so far. I started paying attention to what I would feel and think when she asked me for help. Almost immediately I noticed several things:

- **Excitement,** because helping gave me something to do. My girls were now in school full-time, and I had more time on my hands.
- **Superiority,** because helping her helped me feel better about myself. I liked being the know-it-all; it stroked my ego.

- **Annoyed,** because I had already extended help to her. She should know what to do by now.
- **Disappointment,** because the help I was giving was rarely reciprocated. Was I not worthy of being helped too?
- **Comfort,** because helping was a role I knew well. As a child, I felt loved and most connected to others when I was helpful.

It didn't feel good to acknowledge the part I was playing in this unhealthy cycle. But it was a step in the right direction. And the longer I sat on my hands and paid attention to my old pattern of responses, the more able I was to develop new responses that allowed me to shut down this dysfunctional behavior for good.

I began to feel new things:

- **Discomfort,** because I hated to see my friend in pain. I wasn't good at that. I'm still not.
- **Awkwardness,** because I had to learn new patterns of being in relationship with her and with others. Everything felt so contrived.
- **Grief,** because I ached at letting go of my old ways of helping. They provided me with safety and security. Now I felt naked and exposed.
- **Inferior,** not to her but to God. I had to remember that I am still not him.

The friendship started to settle into a much healthier rhythm, and with the help of boundaries (especially for myself) I began to enjoy our time together again. I no longer enveloped myself into her day-to-day, and I stopped inviting her to be enveloped in mine. My faith was stretched; each time I refused to rely on my old codependent patterns, I was reminded to rely and depend on God instead. When I worried about her, I remembered that God was doing his part to care for her and that she was responsible for herself. When I felt the urge to try to help her, I remembered that this type of help isn't actually helpful. I asked God to help me exercise self-control instead. I no longer looked for this relationship with Ashley to serve me in a way that only held us both back from being who God created us to be. He never needed me to be her messiah, and she was never meant to be mine.

UNHEALTHY OVERLAP

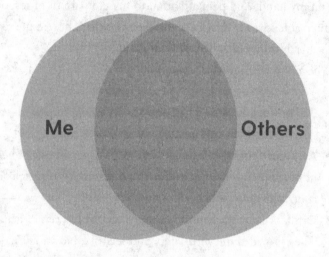

At our core, we were designed to want deep relationships with others, but that becomes a direct reflection of our relationship with God. Codependent patterns in our relationships inhibit our intimacy with our Creator because we draw closer to each other more than to him.

The word *codependency* has increased in popularity in recent decades and in turn has become harder to define. I don't like to label myself (or you) with any one term like *codependent*. Who we are isn't what we have had to do or be. When you acknowledge that you had to use this behavior to feel loved, connected, and safe, you can begin to feel grace and compassion for yourself. This is what is needed to make lasting change—not shame. You can even learn to be grateful for it, since it protected and provided for you when you needed it most. And you can understand now that it is no longer needed. With this heart posture you can slowly take steps toward allowing this behavior to fall by the wayside.

Signs of Codependency

- I feel guilty taking care of myself.
- I feel guilty about success or accomplishments.
- I have low self-esteem and struggle with anxiety.
- I get easily discouraged and overwhelmed.
- I sabotage healthy/safe relationships.
- I tend to remain quiet about my inner suffering and point the attention back to others.
- I lie to myself by believing I am the helpful, sensitive, empathic, responsible one.
- I don't honor red flags.
- I have poor boundaries.
- I am often reactive and later am consumed with shame.
- I don't know who I am without others needing me.
- I don't trust myself, and I don't trust anyone else.
- I fear losing relationships over losing myself.
- I am entirely out of touch with my own needs and wants.
- I defend or justify others' mistreatment of me because it's easier than accepting the truth.
- I don't know how to feel my feelings, so I focus on others' feelings instead.

BIRTHDAY GIFT

I had just had my second daughter, and after over two years of no contact with my parents, my husband and I met them at my therapist's office in an attempt to restore our relationship on new terms. It wasn't easy, meeting in that room with them for the first time. My walls were high, and I didn't feel optimistic about our future. But I knew who God was, and what he was capable of doing wasn't dependent on how I felt about the current circumstances. Plus, he hadn't let me down yet. During those years when I was estranged from my family, he had brought people into my life who didn't replace my parents but people loved on me in maternal and paternal ways I needed most—people who still do to this day. For that I am grateful.

With the help of my therapist, I had been practicing healthy boundary work, mostly centered on developing and exercising self-control. It wasn't about managing others; it was about taking responsibility for myself and my actions. Now, my parents and I would have to find new, healthier ways of connecting outside of what we had always known. It was sort of like dating again, which took time, willingness, and creativity.

Later that year, in December of 2018, I asked my mother for a unique birthday gift. It came in the mail just before my thirty-third birthday. It was a letter I asked her to write to me that detailed her relationship with her own mother, my grandmother. I wasn't sure where our codependency had come from, but I had an idea that it didn't start with me.

I sat down at my desk to open the letter. As I started reading, tears immediately began to stream down my face. It confirmed what I had always known to be true, what God referred to in Exodus when he said, "I lay the sins of the parents upon their children; the entire family is affected—even children in the third and fourth generations of those who reject me" (20:5 NLT).

My mother had been raised in a dysfunctional, broken home. She, too, believed that she had to earn love by managing everyone else's problems and feelings. Her mother did not have a good relationship with her own mother either. My grandmother was raised by a single parent after her father was killed while working as an engineer on a railroad job during the Great Depression. There it all was—*generations of deprivation.*

My mother raised her six younger siblings and recalled that while she had everything she needed, like clothes and food, there was a lack of comfort and love in their home. As a child she always felt like "the help," and she detailed episodes when her mother would retreat to her bedroom for days, even sending her away when her mother lost a child to SIDS.

She described always knowing of her father's infidelity and mentioned her mother leaving for weeks at a time on "vacation," when my mother would be expected to do the laundry, cook the meals, and care for all the other kids. Later, when her parents divorced, she would be responsible for hiring movers and packing up her childhood home alone.

Throughout the five-page letter, she detailed stories of abuse, addiction, lies, and secret keeping, yet she wrote that her mother was "a devout Catholic with a deep faith." She even referred to my grandmother as the strongest woman she knew and the core of their family.

She concluded the letter by admitting that she never saw her mother happy until much later in life when she grew closer to Jesus, her books, and her grandchildren. My mother recalled no memory of any laughter or celebrations, and that as a young child she had learned to just "stay out of the way." Not once did she hear her mother say "I love you"—that is, until her last visit with her in a nursing home, shortly before she passed away.

While I was working to grieve the relationship I thought I had with my mother and accept the one we now had instead, I didn't expect to learn that she, too, was grieving. In my own hurt and disappointment, I never once considered that she was a deprived daughter as well.

Focusing so much on my own pain, I had limited my ability to see hers. Instead, I wanted to blame her. I wanted answers and explanations. I wanted an apology. I wanted a redo. I wanted the mother-daughter relationship I thought my girlfriends had.

I certainly didn't want any of this.

As I put the letter away, I began to see my mother through a different lens. I started to understand that *she did* do better than her own mother had—all while she needed answers, explanations, a redo, and an apology too.

This didn't make reality disappear. It didn't change what had happened and hadn't happened in the past. It did, however, begin to change what was possible for the future. A space in me began to soften, not toward the sin and wrongdoing but toward the woman who, like me, was created in his image.

I've learned several truths:

Children should never have to parent their own parents and siblings.

Children should never have to be their parents' therapist.

Children should never have to worry about who is caring for them.

Children should never have to wonder if they are loved and safe.

Children should never have to sacrifice their childhood.

But my mom didn't know any of that. All she knew was that she had to do what she thought was right at the time for those she loved. She was tormented (physically and verbally) by the people who were meant to provide her protection. She worked hard to preserve her family by shouldering the weight of all the unhealed pain of those before her. This wasn't her pain to carry, but she carried it anyway.

She carried it because that is what she was taught to do for those you loved. It was loyalty to a fault, and *beyond*.

I decided it was time. I was going to end the suffering. I was going to do whatever it took to break free from codependency and heal myself. I was going to do the hard work to break generational cycles of sinning, not just for myself and my own children but for my mother and her mother too.

HIDDEN BELIEFS

I've given you a lot to think about, and you may have more questions than answers right now. That is okay.

Before moving on to practical solutions, I want to discuss the importance of your beliefs. You may have inherited many beliefs about who you are, who others are, and the world around you. Some of these may be untrue, and their lack of truth can be holding you captive.

There isn't a clear, concise path to uprooting your hidden beliefs. But I will share with you what I found to be helpful.

Beliefs/values → thoughts → actions

If you want to better understand what you believe, begin to pay attention to what you think, say, and do. And if you don't like what you are thinking, saying, and doing, then it might be time to change up what you believe.

I began to take note of the times I wanted to say no but said yes instead, and as I did, I found one of the following phrases would be swirling around somewhere in my head.

I am afraid of what they will think.
I am afraid they will get angry.

I am afraid they won't include me.

I am afraid of how they will respond.

I am afraid they will stop loving me.

These thoughts were rooted in hidden beliefs about who I was as a wife, daughter, sister, mother, or friend. Such beliefs are what hold many back from setting healthy and necessary limits. They reinforce the cycle of people-pleasing, performing, and pretending, and in turn keep us bitter and disconnected from others and our authentic selves. More importantly, these hidden beliefs draw you away from living as who God created you to be.

Maybe you can relate to my private coaching client Rebecca, who was asked to host Christmas dinner for her entire extended family. She described feeling the pressure and dealing with it the only way she knew how, by *not* dealing with it. Unfortunately, her inability to say no left her with the unpleasant consequences of this choice. "I felt so anxious, spread thin, and overwhelmed," she told me. As we unpacked her inability to say no, we determined that she was making this choice based on a limiting belief she carried regarding what it meant to be a good daughter. She was fearing how her family would perceive her, and that fear was in control.

The problem with this was that by saying yes when she really needed to say no, she couldn't extend love as she had hoped. The week leading up to Christmas, she was a panicked mess. She spent her afternoons racing around to get groceries and assembling the decor, sniping at her husband and kids, and being unable to sleep. After Christmas was over, it took her weeks to recover from the emotional hangover of it all.

That's because love is never a by-product of fear.

After putting in the work, Rebecca now knows better. She can pause and take some time before defaulting to her normal response of "yes!" when an invite or request comes her way. She can reflect on that experience at Christmas and use it as motivation to challenge her old, hidden beliefs and use self-control for accountability. Today, Rebecca bases her decisions on beliefs that are true for her and who she is in Christ, not ones that are based on lies from the Enemy. She understands that loving others well doesn't mean running herself into the ground. She now knows that she can't serve other people's

That's because love is never a by-product of fear.

opinions and expectations *and* God at the same time. Neither can you.

Rebecca didn't change overnight. It took time for her to integrate and act on her new beliefs about being a "good wife and daughter." Yet as she challenged her hidden beliefs, her thoughts and mindset were directly affected, which left her more equipped to make better decisions for herself in the future. Here, she has a better shot at showing up in her relationships as the loving person she wants to be, void of anxiety, weariness, and resentment. And while she admits to still being a big work in progress, she is taking the necessary steps to make lasting change, most of which include taking personal responsibility for the part she plays in her relationships.

Of course, codependency can't be healed by simply identifying when you want to say no, or uprooting some old, hidden beliefs you carry, but it is a good place to start. Remember, often the hardest boundaries to set are the ones for ourselves, and if our behavior is driven by our beliefs, then our thinking is the conduit.

THINKING ABOUT THOUGHTS

Your thoughts are the conduit between what you believe and what you do.

Read that again.

We have all heard the scriptural command to "take captive every thought" (2 Cor. 10:5). I don't know about you, but I am very literal when it comes to learning, and visualization helps. I imagine myself literally capturing my thoughts inside a little cage. But then what do I do with them once they are there?

We make those thoughts obedient to Christ (2 Cor. 10:5).

We capture them and hold them up to him. It's as if we then say, "Hey, Dad, what do you think of these thoughts of mine? Can I trust them? Are they accurate? Are they true?"

And if not, Paul told us that we have the power within us to demolish them. Every last one of them. But not by our own power. By God's.

Paul, who wrote the letter to the church at Corinth, reminded us that we do not fight the battles of the world the way the world does; instead, we fight with a divine power (2 Cor. 10:4).

Wow, what a gracious God! He tells us, play by play, what to do and how to do it. He even gives us the tools to get it done. Thank you, Lord.

But it is up to us to do what he suggested. We have to think about our thoughts, hold them captive, and lift them to our Father. We then compare the words spiraling around in our heads to the sacred words contained in the Bible. Not just some of the thoughts—every thought. Every claim of the world, every claim we hear on social media, every claim from our mother-in-law, every claim from a friend or teacher, and every claim we think about ourselves. We demolish every claim and argument that sets itself up against the knowledge of God. This is how we hold our thoughts captive and obedient to Christ.

It's a process. It won't happen automatically. It takes effort and energy. But it is so worth the work. Over time, with much patience and practice, you will begin to trust that others will love you, not just when you say yes but even when you say no. (And if they can't, that's okay—we will discuss your options for that later.)

Through thinking more like Christ, we can slowly begin to act more like him too.

- I have a responsibility to think about my thoughts.
- My behavior is an extension of my thinking. God will transform me when I discipline the renewal of my mind (Rom. 12:2).
- Taking my thoughts captive means I have control over them; they don't have control over me.
- At any time I can choose to think more thoughts that are true, noble, right, and pure (Phil. 4:8).
- What I think about will be reflected in how I feel and behave, and these feelings and behaviors will then reinforce the ways I think.
- God's Spirit is in me; I have the power to disable any thoughts and to focus on thoughts that are obedient to him.

ACKNOWLEDGE & CONFRONT

1. Review the signs of codependency. Do you identify with any?
2. Who before you modeled codependency?
3. Is your well-being or mood currently dependent on someone else's? Describe that relationship and if there are any boundaries present.
4. Do you have a hard time saying no because of a hidden belief about what it means to be a good daughter, wife, sister, coworker, or friend? Explain.
5. How would holding your thoughts captive allow you to exercise more self-control in your relationships?

PART 2

Practical Solutions

BOUNDARY WORK IS QUITE LITERALLY GOD'S work. In the very beginning we see this with his original design, both his love and his limits, partnered together. When you choose to use boundaries with yourself and in your relationships, you will begin to experience an abundance of blessings, like confidence and peace. You will also become more clearheaded and far more equipped. The energy you used to expend on others' problems becomes energy you use to fulfill your purpose and his kingdom work. Here you are better positioned to take his lead rather than to manufacture a path of your own.

Sometimes you will have to fight the urge to go back to your old ways of manufacturing a sense of safety, acceptance, or connection through your own will or creativity. Remember, God created love not just for us to use on others but so we can love him *first*. He doesn't want you producing love from some temporary source, because he knows that won't fulfill or sustain you. We can dwell inside safe, wholesome relationships, but apart from him that is not possible. He is the Vine; we are simply the branches. Our integrity relies on being close to him, and when we aren't, everything suffers (John 15:4).

God created love not just for us to use on others but so we can love him *first*.

While love is a precious gift, we need self-control and boundaries to love others the way God intended us to. Learning new, healthy patterns requires discipline, which is what will change your heart over time, and not the other way around. It is often a rewiring of thinking and behavior that involves returning to him before anyone or anything else.

My hope is that, throughout this next section, you will learn to no longer fear limits within your relationships and within yourself, but instead you will long for them. As image bearers of God, we can reflect his nature and character *through* our relationships, which will happen only when we begin to observe the limits set by God *for* our relationships. But, friend, this opportunity is worth celebrating. The good news is that when you establish this habit of returning to his love first, you reap the reward of receiving and gifting love in the way God intended you to.

7

What Is a Boundary?

WHEN OUR TWO OLDEST DAUGHTERS WERE toddlers, we began giving them vitamins. Of course, these weren't just any vitamins; they were the fruit-shaped, colorful kind that tasted really good. Every night before bed we would give them each one, leaving my husband and me to pat ourselves on the back for being such great parents.

Fast-forward two years, to an afternoon when I was sitting alongside my daughter as she had her first checkup with a pediatric dentist. The dentist looked over at me and said, "Mom, she has quite a few cavities. Has she been eating a lot of dried fruits or candy?"

I cringed. My face felt flush, my body tense. I began to brace for what was coming next. "No, we rarely eat candy . . . some raisins on occasion. But, wait, she does take gummy vitamins. Could that be why?"

And, sure enough, that was most likely the culprit. Apparently the residue of the gummy vitamins would sit on her teeth each night, eroding away at her enamel. This enamel is the toughest tissue found in the human body, but it still didn't stand a chance with the gummy texture lodged into each crevice. Night after night those tasty gummies wreaked havoc on my baby's teeth, and I was to blame.

For days I was unable to sleep. I felt so much guilt. How could I not have known? Why didn't I ever think for one second that this would cause so much harm? Wasn't it obvious? I felt like the worst mother ever.

Then, early one morning as I lay in bed, I felt a rush of warmth run through my body and a loud, almost audible phrase come through: *Forgive yourself.* It had to have come from God because the last thing I was considering was letting myself off the hook for being such a crappy caregiver. But I decided to press into the idea, because I was tired of letting this eat away at me. What was done was done, and I was ready to move on. I could ensure that we made it to each of her next three appointments to get every cavity filled and sealed, and toss the gummy vitamins, but there wasn't much else I could do.

A lot of times this is what we do in our relationships. We sometimes think we are doing the right thing, the best thing, the helpful thing that makes us feel secure and good, yet before we know it, we look up and that seemingly good thing has turned into a bad thing. And perhaps, like me, you never saw it coming.

But you, too, can choose to take the next right step. You don't have to live paralyzed or afraid or uncertain. You can forgive yourself because you are human and allow yourself some self-compassion. You don't have to live ashamed of doing what you thought was best at the time. You can consider where to pivot next, then move on, putting new boundaries in place. This is the process of life.

FOR YOUR OWN GOOD

One of my favorite definitions of a boundary is from Dr. Henry Cloud, author of the world-famous book *Boundaries.* He writes that "a boundary shows me where I end and someone else begins, leading me to a sense of ownership."

Again, boundaries are created by and for God. They are a part of his plan for our protection and provision. God sets limits to ensure that he stays at the center of our lives; otherwise, we tend to place other things there instead. It is why we see boundaries throughout both the Old and New Testaments, from God dividing the land from the sea to working six days and choosing to rest on the seventh. We see it when he teaches that we will reap what we sow. We see it through his instruction to seek wisdom and to practice both discernment and self-control. Scripture is doused with boundary work.

You and I were created in God's image, and this design comes with limits. For many, the idea of limits can seem suffocating or controlling. This, I believe, is because many have had an experience with limits or discipline that was either abusive or unhealthy, whether in their childhoods, marriages, jobs, friendships, or within themselves. This bad experience has left them to toss out the idea altogether, and this develops into a problem of its own. I encourage you to remember that your bad experience with a boundary doesn't make boundary work a bad thing; it's the human error found within it that does.

It is easy to confuse limit setting with rules and control. Yet we see in Mark 2:27 that while the religious people were defining different regulations to keep the Sabbath, God reassured them that the Sabbath was made for their benefit. This is what God does. He sets limits for our advantage, and our part is rejecting some of our own autonomy to embrace a dependence on him.

It is important that we begin to reframe limits as a blessing by God, for God, and for us. When we approach a boundary practice with this in mind, it becomes easier to use this practice as a gift we have received from our Creator, one that we can and should generously pour out in our relationships.

Maintaining a biblical perspective when practicing boundaries is also crucial to keep what the world thinks about your limits in check. Whenever you begin to feel guilty or selfish, you may need to pause and evaluate whether you are slipping back into a pattern that is unhealthy. A worldly perspective will have you—not God—at the center of your relationships. It will reaffirm that you can and should pursue happiness and comfort over wholeness and discomfort. It will try to convince you that you can actually fix a situation or save a person from their own problems. But boundary work is godly work, and becoming more like God starts by knowing you aren't him—so keep that close.

Only by understanding fully that boundaries are for your own good will you be able to set them with confidence. Guilt cannot exist in your obedience to his Word.

Obeying God's limits → limits through self-control → limits within relationships

Many assume that boundaries cause pain and disconnection within relationships. My inbox is flooded daily with messages written by women (usually empty nesters) who are hurt and confused by this whole boundary business.

"You are the reason my daughter is no longer talking to me!"

"How dare you destroy families with this stuff. Shame on you!"

"Boundaries are the most selfish thing I have ever heard of."

"How can a person really just cut off someone they love? Unreal!"

I gently remind some of these women that boundaries don't destroy families—sin does. A relationship void of boundaries is usually a relationship filled with anxiety, anger, and resentment. A healthy relationship will never crumble under the weight of healthy boundaries. In fact, healthy boundaries are the foundation on which healthy relationships are built.

RESENTMENT

Resentment is the leading silent killer within our closest relationships and is the by-product of a relationship without limits.

Resentment is

- negative thoughts;
- fear or avoidance of a person who has disappointed or hurt you;
- feelings of anger, frustration, or irritability toward someone who has wronged you;
- bitterness that you haven't been treated fairly; and
- an inability to stop thinking about what happened.[1]

During my research on resentment, I came across this and found it rather helpful in understanding the cycle resentment plays on our hearts and minds. The word *resentment* originates from the French root word *ressentir*.

The prefix *re-* means "again."

And *sentir* means "to feel."[2]

Essentially, to live resentfully is to "re-feel," over and over. Many don't know they are living with resentment, but the body can feel it. In fact, physical damage can come from living with resentment. Dr. Carsten Wrosch, of Concordia University in Montreal, explains that "resentment and bitterness interfere with our body's hormonal systems. This causes a damaging effect through our entire body, much like extreme stress." Dr. Wrosch has noted that these negative emotions interfere with our immune system as well, causing us to be susceptible to illness and disease.[3]

It appears that when we live with resentment, not only is it silently killing our relationships, but it causes harm to our physical bodies in the process.

Why Do We Get Resentful?

When we are dishonest with ourselves, we fall into the trap of assuming that we are the only ones who can do for others what they can't or won't do for themselves. Then we blame others for our lack of limits, and we exercise no self-control. The thoughts of *this is how it's always been* or *this is how it will always be* take up space in our heads. We settle for the victim role and don't claim ownership over our part in neglecting to set and maintain limits. Worst of all, we believe the lie that we must remain loyal to a fault to love others well.

How Do We Break Free from It?

We break free from resentment by taking radical responsibility for ourselves. If our relationships suck, we take half the blame, no more, no less. When we feel resentment creep in, we can engage in an honest dialogue with ourselves and God about what we can and should be doing in our relationships. How are the responsibilities being distributed? Are our needs being met? How is the ongoing reciprocity? You see, when we have a hard conversation with ourselves first, we can then choose to have a hard conversation about our limits with someone else. And here something brave and powerful happens, something that really annoys the Enemy . . . we turn *toward* each other, not away. Resentment leaves us disconnected and hurt, but boundaries allow us to fight for our relationships.

- We begin to get radically honest and responsible with ourselves and allow others to be responsible for themselves.
- We start exercising self-control and set strong limits on ourselves first.
- We begin to think and act from a new belief that says, "I can change, and so can my relationships."
- We no longer settle for being a victim, blaming others for our resentment.

- We avoid living loyal to a fault by establishing a healthy boundary practice.

Something else happens when you decide not to live resentfully (yes, it is a conscious choice). You begin to unequivocally let others off the hook for your happiness. This is how patterns of behavior, like codependency, are stopped in their tracks. When you unhook others, you simultaneously unhook yourself. No longer are you expecting yourself to be their source of happiness, health, or wellness. Slowly, everyone settles into their natural and rightful place, and boundaries do their job to keep you there. These boundaries ensure that you don't overstep as the control freak or under-step as the victim. They ensure that you don't ask yourself to keep me happy and you don't expect me to keep you happy.

But it isn't always easy.

We already took some time to work through issues in your family of origin as well as uproot any hidden beliefs you have driving your existing dysfunctional patterns of thinking and behavior. Now it is time to identify your core values. These will be the motivation and foundation on which you establish your boundary practice.

> **When you decide not to live resentfully, you begin to unequivocally let others off the hook for your happiness.**

CORE VALUES

After teaching boundary work for almost a decade, I conducted a poll in the spring of 2020 to ask my community on social media if they were able to identify their core values; 74 percent said no. This made me realize I had been skipping over a valuable and essential piece of this work. You must be able to fully identify your core values before setting any sort of boundary, because this is what anchors you to yourself.

Core values are the foundation your life is built on, and are the driving force behind how you think, feel, and behave. When you are clear about your core values, you can become clear on what boundaries you need to guard them. Not knowing what your core values are can leave you exposed to the risk of believing, defending, or advocating for things that are simply what those around you believe, defend, and advocate for. This is a common cause for confusion, exhaustion, and anxiety. When you know what you value, you can find confidence and peace internally, as opposed to externally.

If your core values aren't clear, then you won't have a home base to return to. This is important because without one you might be tempted to return to unhealthy relationships or patterns of behavior that reflect some sense of pseudosafety instead.

You may also reflect and see that your earliest caregivers valued things that never should have been valued and were empty pursuits. It is important to spend time deciding for yourself what you value, because if you don't, those before you or the world around you will do it for you.

Please be aware that some values will change as your life's seasons change. For example, you may not have a clear value on your standards of education, but after becoming a mother, that shifts. Or perhaps you have never thought of yourself as frugal, but when you graduate from college and begin paying your own bills, you realize frugality suddenly has value. This is normal. Core values don't have to be set in stone, yet having *evolving* core values is not the same as having *unclear* core values.

WHAT ARE MY CORE VALUES?

Some gospel values are nonnegotiables. These values are usually a reflection of how you live and behave because you follow Jesus. They don't come naturally but rather are the by-products of being transformed, nurtured, and sustained by God's Spirit. These include many of the fruits we learn about in Scripture, including patience, peace, and self-control.

Still, other values are deeply woven into the tapestry of our lives. These values may seem less subtle, but they pack a major punch long-term. They may differ from household to household; however, these differences don't mean they are wrong—they just mean they are different. We can and should respect each other's values whenever possible, without aborting our own.

Consider the healthy relationships you are working to establish. These relationships will be secured in part by the behavior you elicit, which will be determined by your core values. As the Bible says in Luke 6:48, you build your life on solid rock. Here you can begin to reverse engineer your legacy with intention, because the impact you are making in this life is a direct result of how you influence the lives of others.

Knowing your core values will help you take more responsibility for your actions, which will require you to set better boundaries.

You can ask yourself these questions:

- **Who am I?** (A child of Christ.)
- **What do I value?** (This should reflect your identity in Christ.)
- **How can I establish better habits and behaviors that reflect what I value?** (Your identity drives your activity.)
- **How will I use boundaries to guard these new behaviors and, ultimately, what I value?** (This reinforces both what you value and the behavior.)

- **How will this process help me to actively write my legacy?**
  (core values → reflected in your behavior → influences your
  relationships good or bad → affects your legacy forever)

When I first began identifying my values, I started with my marriage. I began to notice that the world's standards didn't value it in the same regard that God asked me to. More specifically, I had a coworker who would constantly complain about her husband, and I, too, would fall into the trap of belittling my husband alongside her. We would complain about what appeared to be harmless things, until one day God revealed to me something different. On days I worked with her, I found myself bringing home this same kind of garbage talk to my husband, saying things that were both disrespectful and degrading. I didn't have a clear value around guarding my marriage, and this lack of clarity is why a coworker was able to infiltrate our union. Our behavior wasn't so harmless after all.

I asked myself if these conversations actually aligned with the core values I wanted for my marriage. And they did not, even though my behavior said otherwise. Once I became clear on my core value in honoring my marriage through respecting my husband, I was able to alter my behavior, which meant disengaging from this sort of talk. This change did two things: it supported my core value by reinforcing what I already believed but was not yet acting on and it guarded my marriage, which I value dearly.

My core value → drives my behavior → which affects those around me

Now, let's look at this from a different perspective. Let's say I chose not to identify a core value around marriage. It would be very possible for my value to then be influenced and determined by my unassuming coworker, which in turn would affect my behavior. The complaining itself seemed harmless, but over time it would develop into how I viewed my marriage or, worse, how I spoke to and treated my husband. This would affect how he felt about himself, how he behaved at work, and how we as a married couple treated our children. This all comes as a result of not taking responsibility for my core values.

Coworker's core value → drives my behavior
→ affects my marriage → reinforces
what I value about my marriage

Listen, I get it. Sometimes it isn't easy to value different things from those around you. You may be judged, left out, or teased for putting first what others put last. Expect that, over time, as you learn to value what God values, your close circle will change. Know that this isn't personal, and God will bless you for standing faithful through this season of discomfort.

"Seek first his kingdom and his righteousness, and all these things will be given to you as well" (Matt. 6:33).

ACKNOWLEDGE & CONFRONT

1. Have you ever felt like you were doing something helpful, but in the end it wasn't helpful after all? Explain.

2. Is there a relationship you are in right now that would benefit from a healthy boundary? Describe how this boundary might serve as both protection and provision for you.

3. Are you currently carrying a resentment? What would happen if you got radically honest with yourself about the part you are playing in the continued suffering?

4. Identify your core values. Take some time now to write down three.

5. Do these core values currently align with your behavior? How will what you value affect and influence those around you?

8

Communication Styles

"IT DOESN'T HAPPEN ALL THE TIME," SHE SAID.
"But when it does, it's bad."

"How bad is *bad*?" I asked.

"Well, I usually lose my cool and blow up. I may throw the TV clicker or slam a cabinet door. Then I snap at my husband and the kids and go to bed feeling so ashamed. Sometimes we don't talk for hours about what happened, days even."

"And what happens when you do finally talk?" I asked.

"We pretend like nothing happened."

Julie was a longtime, founding member of Discover Your Worth. She had joined because she was starting to wonder if having boundaries would help her feel less exhausted and angry as a wife and mother. During her onboarding period, she worked through her family of origin inventory and found that in her childhood she witnessed a lot of conflict that was aggressive in nature. While no one was physically hurt during these disagreements, she often felt unsafe because of the words spoken and, more so, *how* they were spoken.

Fast-forward, and she has now found herself ill-equipped to communicate in an effective way. She shared with me that she often would let "little" offenses build up, such as her husband not helping with the household chores or her mother-in-law commenting in a snarky tone to her at dinner, and then *bam!* She would explode in rage, saying and doing things she would later regret. "It's as if I don't see it coming. Then I feel like I am racing to clean up the mess I made, and I see that my kids are beginning to feel scared of my outbursts. They're just as confused as me, but I don't know how to stop."

Julie's situation is not uncommon. In fact, it is a clear example of just how powerful unhealthy communication styles observed in childhood can be. These methods are likely to be passed down, even if you swear to yourself you would never speak or act like those who came before you. But please be encouraged—the very fact that you learned this behavior means you can now unlearn it.

PASSIVE, AGGRESSIVE, PASSIVE-AGGRESSIVE

Before we start to practice healthy communication, I want you to first understand the three styles of unhealthy communication to avoid: *passive*, *aggressive*, and *passive-aggressive*. As you review these, you will likely find one style you can most identify with, because it is what you witnessed most frequently as a child. Taking time to acknowledge this is important, not to cast blame but to use this knowledge for much-needed change. By default, we tend to do things the way our parents or caregivers did. Becoming aware of these patterns of behavior will allow you to keep what you want and dispose of what you don't.

Perhaps you witnessed parents who engaged in communicating through conflict in ways that involved door-slamming, name-calling, or yelling. Maybe you had a parent avoid conflict by disappearing or giving the silent treatment when tension rose. Maybe you felt uncertain about conflict in general, but you do remember knowing when and how to pretend like things were okay even when everyone knew they weren't. Whatever it was, you began to fear conflict because it conveyed to you that you weren't safe. In order to set healthy boundaries, you can learn to practice healthy communication through healthy confrontation and conflict.

Passive: The Question Mark (?)

Passive communication is confusing and questionable. It is communicating in a way that works to secure some sense of agreement, approval, or acceptance. As a child you may have witnessed a parent who appeared on the outside as a "go with the flow" type. Yet as you matured, you began to see this as a reflection of their own self-degradation and lack of confidence.

At its core, passive communication is self-serving. It's a way to secure control by avoiding conflict and working instead to keep the peace. When we avoid conflict, we manufacture some form of temporary relief from the discomfort, but we never get to the root of the problem. Passivity avoids vulnerability, and without vulnerable communication we can never authentically be connected, which is why distrust grows. Chronic passivity erodes your ability to stand up for yourself or to speak up for what you need. This is in part due to constantly being distracted by what those around you are doing, thinking, and needing.

For example, you have a coworker who comes to visit your office every day during her lunch hour. While you'd much rather have this time to yourself, you allow her to barge in time and time again to vent about her current affairs. This bothers you, but you remain passive to it all because you don't want to hurt her feelings. You believe listening to her is helpful and considerate, so you stuff your needs away.

LOYAL TO A FAULT

Aggressive: The Exclamation Point (!)

Aggressive communication is explosive and erratic. At its core, it is an attempt to secure control through aggression or manipulation. If you can be loud, then maybe you can be heard, or so you think. And if you can be heard, you have a better shot at changing the circumstance. You may have witnessed a caregiver yelling to get her point across or to try to force some sort of stability in an otherwise unstable situation. Perhaps she feared she was losing authority and worked to get it back through threats or coercion. Due to its unpredictable nature it, too, fosters distrust.

For example, my DYW member Julie—whom I referred to earlier—described her house being a mess, her children demanding a snack, and her husband walking in after work to turn on a football game and kick back in his recliner. This would happen day after day until she couldn't take it anymore, and she would explode. She would tell me that before she began practicing healthy confrontation with assertive communication, she would yell at her kids, sending them upstairs to bed early and leaving dinner uncooked on the stove, and retreat to her room for solace. This cycle never allowed her to get to the root problem (feeling underappreciated and exhausted) and instead only added to it.

Passive-Aggressive: The Uncertain Irritability (?!)

Passive-aggressive communication comes across as the more likable of the three unhealthy styles, and because of this, it can fly under the radar much longer. It is a blend of both passive (uncertainty) and aggressive (irritability) and is what I consider to be the "backdoor approach" of communicating. It usually arises because someone is unpleased or disappointed yet unable to really identify those feelings head-on, let alone communicate them. At its root, the desire is to control another person or outcome indirectly with comments that have you perplexed or working hard to read between the lines. Perhaps it is a snarky comment or a statement that leaves you wondering, *Wait— what did they just mean by that?*

Take Karen, for example. She calls to tell her mother that she has made the decision not to make the trip home this year for the holidays. Her mother at first sounds understanding; however, Karen later sees her mother's posts on social media, that say "This holiday season will not be the same without my daughter. I don't know how I will manage!" and an influx of little memes, including one where it appears to be a crying grandmother surrounded by buzzing broken hearts. The posts are then flooded with comments from women on Karen's mother's pickleball team sympathizing with her pain: "Oh no, how could she?" and "I can't believe she would miss out on precious time with you!"

Passive-aggressive communication avoids the problem and, like the others, adds unnecessary confusion and tension to an already difficult situation. In most cases this communication style comes from people who can't deal with their own feelings. It is a habitual way for them to let off steam and secure relief from their feelings without taking responsibility for them. Even though passive-aggressive communication can be indirect, this does not soften the destruction on a relationship. Many who are on the receiving end of this communication style can feel enticed to withdraw or to respond in a similar passive-aggressive nature.

WHAT IS HEALTHY COMMUNICATION?

While unhealthy communication can leave you with vague question marks, alarming exclamation marks, and confusing combinations, healthy communication is always clear. Using assertive communication does two things that the other two do not: it leaves space for vulnerability, and it actively surrenders control.

Remember, vulnerability is the key to showing up in your relationships with honesty. This comes first by having an honest chat with yourself about what is going on in your head and heart. It sets aside pretending for the sake of keeping the peace. It doesn't hide behind anger to get its way. And it never chooses to use a joke or backhanded comment to manipulate or control. It courageously allows you to take continued personal responsibility before self-imploding or exploding by being forthcoming about what you actually need. It works to foster safety, trust, and accountability in your relationships in a kind and clear way.

Passive, aggressive, and passive-aggressive communication all have this one thing in common: they strive to secure some form of dominance over a person or outcome. But assertive communication releases the need for control over and over again. It is a way that you can pour back into your relationships and is an outward expression that fear isn't in charge. You see, as a Christian, you don't actually need to control others because you know who controls all things (Ps. 22:28). Instead, you choose to exercise self-control; after all, *you* are the only one you can control anyway.

> **As a Christian, you don't actually need to control others because you know who controls all things.**

Assertive: The Period (.)

Assertive communication is the healthy method of communication you will want to work toward using consistently. It is clear, confident, and kind, not filled with questions, anger, or sarcasm. It kicks fear out of the driver's seat and allows you full responsibility for how you interact with others. Your words are rooted in firmly knowing and guarding your core values, and they work to support and reinforce your new healthy behavior.

Assertive communication does not take shortcuts or back doors to get a point across. It asks honest questions to try to better understand others and is genuinely held up by a higher purpose: knowing that our words have power to speak life into our relationships (Prov. 18:21). As Dr. Henry Cloud says, "Assertive communication is choosing to go hard on the problem and easy on the other person."[1]

Let's revisit my previous examples and swap out the unhealthy methods for an assertive example of communicating.

Passive Reframe: The Coworker During Lunch

You have finally admitted to yourself that while you respect and care for your coworker Jess, you really would prefer to limit the amount of time she visits you during your lunch break. You are learning how to make nice with your own needs, too, and you realize that you aren't serving this relationship well because you're avoiding the necessary confrontation required to express a healthy limit.

Knock knock. The door cracks open and in pops your coworker's head. "Hey, it's me. Do you have a minute?" she asks.

In a calm yet confident tone, you may reply something like, "Actually, Jess, I don't today. In fact, I would rather us schedule our lunches together. Let's look at the calendar now and see what day works later in the month."

This reframe allows you to communicate that your needs also matter and that when you value your own time, those around you will too. It also gives you an opportunity to be a supportive and caring friend to Jess, lending an ear when it is conducive to you. Maybe it's just once a week, or semimonthly, or once a month. But you get to decide, not your fears or her expectations. Here, you build trust back up by guarding your time and needs, and Jess learns to trust you with your word. She knows that when you do meet at the designated time, you will be *all in*. The truth is that no one wants to be burdensome. Boundaries allow you to honor what you both need, while pouring into the relationship the love, respect, and time it deserves.

By communicating passively, one hopes that a problem will suddenly resolve on its own, get better with time, or slowly dissipate. But as most of us have experienced, avoiding a problem doesn't make the problem go away. Assertive communication allows you the opportunity to be vulnerable and honest while taking responsibility, all of which are essential in establishing quality relationships. You can express your wants and needs while also considering the wants and needs of others. Boundaries give you this flexibility and freedom.

Aggressive Reframe: Julie at Home

DYW member Julie took some time to get to the root of the unmet need she had. Her aggression and irritability were simply a symptom of her attempts at getting that need met, both through coercion and control. Julie admitted that she wanted to feel more appreciated and helped by her partner, and she had hoped that he would catch on after her outbursts. I gently reminded her that it was possible to feel appreciated and to receive more support at home, but she would have to take responsibility for her part in practicing assertive communication about what that actually looked like before she unraveled. After all, her partner couldn't read her mind, and it was unkind and unfair to assume so.

Julie was able to identify that she needed to speak up—when her chest started to tighten or her breath shortened. "I could feel a sort of temper tantrum coming on," she told me. When this signal happened, I encouraged her to pause and ask herself, *What do I need in this moment to feel supported?*

The answer to this held so much power, and what she did with that answer took a ton of vulnerability. Sometimes it sounded like "Hey, honey, can you wait to watch your show? How about taking the kids out front to play so I can start dinner?" At other times it was more direct. "I need help tidying the countertops because the clutter leaves me feeling overwhelmed. Let's take a few minutes to go through this paperwork and mail." And on other occasions she even let him take the reins by bidding for connection. "How about a date later this week? Can you ask your mom to babysit? I am open to whatever you plan!" It didn't always look the same, but it resulted in a similar benefit. It also didn't always happen perfectly, but over time she did report on the many benefits of practicing a kind, clear, and consistent communication style. Her husband felt more helpful and respected; she felt more helped and loved. There was much more ease where tension once resided, and their kids were blessed by observing this assertive communication.

Passive-Aggressive Reframe: Mother and the Holidays

Karen is beginning to spot a consistent pattern of passive-aggressive communication between her and her mother. She realizes that while she can't control what her mother says and does, she can control how she will respond and at what level she will tolerate this type of communication in their relationship. Karen takes some time to process what her mother's comments bring up: hurt, embarrassment, and anger. She gives it a few days so that the emotions can subside, then gives her mother a call directly.

The phone rings and she picks up.

"Hello?"

"Hey, Mom, after we spoke last week about me not coming home for the holidays, I saw online that you posted about our conversation. I also see that your friends are now commenting about it. This doesn't change me not coming, but it does upset me to see our personal discussions shared online. Can we talk about this?"

While Karen may not have the perfect words, she is working to use assertive communication to bring about clarity in an otherwise unclear and difficult situation. She is taking responsibility for her own part, trying to approach the problem head-on before it causes more problems down the road.

"Oh, Karen, you are just being too sensitive!" her mother replies.

Karen now has a choice. She can either react to this comment with the anger and disappointment that is bubbling up by saying something unkind and hanging up, or she can take authority over those emotions and get curious. What is it her mother is hoping to gain by her passive-aggressive comments? What is it *she* needs? And how can Karen work to meet that while not sacrificing her own needs in the process?

Karen's mother may never admit to Karen directly that she is hurt, or that she is sad because she misses Karen after she moved across the country a few years back. Karen's mother may never have the skill set to engage in healthy, assertive communication, and she may never be willing to put forth the same amount of energy and effort Karen is into their relationship. But Karen can still pursue the necessary confrontation, no matter how uncomfortable, because this relationship matters to her. The more practice she gets at handling tension in a healthy way, the less fearful she will become and the less likely she will allow that fear to dictate her behavior. Here, she can lean on the safety found in using her new skill and not on her old ways of managing conflict.

Remember, choosing to practice this style of communicating is simply an open invitation for others to use it with you. But there are no guarantees they will. Part of the work will be learning how to let go of the outcome and choosing to do only what you can do. It will also mean learning how to practice safe conflict with those who are willing to play by the same rules. At times this may mean surrendering to what you had hoped the relationship would become and instead accepting what it is right now. You can rest in the peace of knowing that you are doing your part (no more, no less) to bridge the gap between their needs and yours through assertive, healthy communication.

ACKNOWLEDGE & CONFRONT

1. What holds you back from assertively communicating in your relationships? Explain.
2. Which of the three communication styles (passive, aggressive, or passive-aggressive) did you most witness in your childhood?
3. Which of the three communication styles do you default to as an adult woman now? Share a recent example of when you poorly communicated.
4. What *unmet need* were you trying to communicate (appreciation, respect, love, support, space, consideration, etc.)?
5. If you could go back and assertively communicate, how would that sound? Detail a dialogue.

9

Conflict

BECOMING BETTER AT ASSERTIVE COMMUNICA-
tion requires us to become better skilled at engaging in healthy
conflict. Healthy conflict isn't responsible for why loving people do
unloving things; avoiding conflict is.

> **When we choose not to confront the issues in front of us, we are choosing to remain a part of the problem.**

Avoiding conflict is in part why many people remain passive victims to unhealthy relationships or circumstances. When we choose not to confront the issues in front of us, we are choosing to remain a part of the problem. We have all experienced it—something that seems so trivial over time snowballing into a much bigger issue.

Living with any sort of avoidance mentality keeps you pointing the finger at everyone else, blaming them for the fact that you continue to be so unhappy. Again, this provides some temporary relief, but long-term you will never maintain healthy relationships if you don't take personal responsibility for your part in them. Healthy conflict is the key to healthy connection and personal growth.

What's So Hard About Confrontation?

In order to engage in healthy conflict, you must become more comfortable with facing confrontation head-on. Perhaps when you were growing up, confrontation looked and sounded scary. You don't want to feel unsafe like that again, so bobbing and weaving your way around conflict has become a suitable alternative.

To begin setting healthy boundaries, you will start by first leaning into safe conflict.

This can be found through engaging in conflict with people who are playing by the same "rules" of healthy confrontation as you. These rules include respectful tone and talk, kind body language, and honesty. They also include an established sense of trust that promises not to abandon you when any sort of healthy conflict arises. Fear of losing connection is at the root of why many people avoid conflict entirely. This practice will be made available to you through identifying safe relationships that are established over time, which I will touch on in a later chapter.

Since none of us really like to confront each other, we don't. But the less we do it, the less practice we get, and the less practice we get, the less we receive the benefit of it. This is why we never truly appreciate confrontation for the value it has in serving our healthy relationships, so the avoiding continues.

Confrontation within conflict is also difficult because we tend to listen to a lie that is on repeat inside our heads. This lie tends to sound like this:

I have to let this go or I will lose them.
It isn't worth the fight.
I am probably just overreacting.
I need to just forget about it and move on.

Imagine for a moment that for months you have been putting in extra hours at the office, preparing for an upcoming presentation. You finalize the last detail and have a coworker review it before presenting it to your boss.

The morning of the presentation is here. To your dismay, the same coworker you had look over your presentation now interrupts you, taking credit for your hard work. Rather than speak up, you nervously smile, avoiding any sort of confrontation, and "play nice" instead.

How did a lie interfere with your ability to confront your coworker?

Most likely you were choosing to believe something that sounded like, "You won't seem like a team player if you make a scene about this," which left you withdrawing from an opportunity to assert yourself. Or you thought, *What's the big deal? She did provide me important feedback.* But this lie led you to avoid, and that avoidance has you resenting your coworker as more unresolved issues begin to pile up. *Maybe I will start looking for another job that appreciates me more*, you begin to think.

Here is the deal: you may find another job, but the same pattern and problem will arise. That's because the problem isn't that your job doesn't appreciate you. It's that *you* don't appreciate you, and your lack of boundaries shows. These lies can slowly become truth in our heads if we let them, and this is how they begin to control our behavior and communication.

Change won't happen overnight. An easy starting point is

deciding today to no longer blame others for your lack of limits and choosing instead to confront issues that need confronting, no matter how scary. It also helps by remembering that confrontation or expressing your healthy limits is not unkind, unloving, or selfish. By turning toward the tension and not away from it, you commit to being a part of the solution and no longer remaining a part of the problem.

CHECK YOUR MOTIVES

Knowing your motives before confronting an issue is extremely important. Many of the women who come to work with me believe they are rightly motivated when they approach setting a boundary. But once we begin to unpack their feelings and thoughts behind it, they realize they were not fueled by healthy motives, and the confrontation is less productive than they had hoped. Healthy confrontation is the result of leaning in when the discomfort arises, with healthy motives as support.

By turning toward the tension and not away from it, you commit to being a part of the solution and no longer remaining a part of the problem.

If you find yourself scrambling or reacting impulsively, you aren't engaging in healthy conflict, and most likely you are unclear on your motives. Boundaries that are communicated through healthy confrontation are well-thought-out in both motivation and delivery.

UNHEALTHY MOTIVES	HEALTHY MOTIVES
To control or manage others' behavior	To communicate how you want to be spoken to
To attempt to fix, save, or rescue others	To help you feel safe in your mind and body
To seek revenge or payback	To guard your core values, time, talents, or gifts
To manipulate	To protect your privacy and progress
To get attention or cause drama	To keep the bad out, and to keep you in

ROADBLOCKS

There are certain statements that can prevent you from setting a boundary through healthy confrontation, yet they can be harder to identify, as they can very much be factual. These "roadblocks" may be shared by well-intending people (friends or family members who just want to see you happy) and not just by those who are used to getting their way through manipulation or guilt. Be on the lookout for both.

These are the most common roadblocks:

"But they are family!"
"You are being too sensitive."
"Do you think you are better than us now?"
"You just don't know how to have any fun."
"I was only kidding!"
"Life is short, just forgive and move on."
"Everyone is human and makes mistakes."

After hearing one of these, you may want to revert to an old pattern of people-pleasing or pretending. You may begin to elicit some codependent traits that have you putting your wants or needs last. You may feel tempted to harbor resentment, again. At the very least you will likely avoid setting a much-needed boundary.

As I said, some of these statements may be facts. They may *be* family; life *is* very short. Everyone *does* make mistakes. But their factual essence doesn't change another fact: *a boundary needs to be communicated.*

God didn't create you to be a doormat. He wants you to thrive inside healthy relationships. He has a purpose for you and wants to fuel you with the passion to live it out. But you must guard yourself from believing a lie or becoming controlled by a roadblock that throws you off the healthy new path you are headed down. You can learn to spot these roadblocks for what they are, and you can choose to pursue the next step toward no longer fearing healthy confrontation.

If you find yourself in a situation where a roadblock is suddenly hurled your way, return to these important reminders for encouragement:

- I can spot a lie or roadblock and choose to no longer apologize for, justify, or defend my limits.
- I can be compassionate toward others without being swept away by their chaos or problems.
- I can hold safe space for others while remembering it isn't my job to step in and fix everything.
- I can love someone and limit how much I expose myself to them.
- I can discern to whom I allow access to me, and how much, without guilt.
- I can guard my emotional capacity and still be a great wife, mother, sister, daughter, and friend.

As author Lysa TerKeurst says, "I don't draw boundaries hoping to force another person to change in ways they may be unwilling to change or incapable of changing. Instead, I place boundaries on *myself* to help me exercise self-control over what I will and will not tolerate."[1]

As you practice healthy confrontation, roadblocks will no longer derail, distract, or discourage you. They cease to have the power to throw you off course. You know where you are headed, and you no longer second-guess yourself or your needs. You begin to cling to your core values and guard them, even if that means disagreeing with others and engaging in healthy confrontation. You may still worry about what others think or how they will respond, but you won't allow this to control how you show up for yourself and for your relationships.

AVOIDING CONFLICT IN HARD SEASONS

You may be wondering if there is ever a "not so good" time for confrontation in your relationships. This is a common question I get, especially if the confrontation you need to have is with a person who is going through an especially hard season. He is suffering from an illness. She lost her job. Her husband left her for another woman. His kid just had emergency surgery.

There is no easy way to sugarcoat this. So I won't try to.

Your not setting a boundary during someone's hard season just makes their season *harder*.

I think that when we hold off on setting a limit, or when we curb our approach,

> **Your not setting a boundary during someone's hard season just makes their season *harder*.**

we hope it will make a complicated situation less complicated. Unfortunately the opposite happens.

There is never a good, convenient, or easy time to have a hard conversation. But we can try to remember that when someone is going through a rough season of unpredictability, anxiety, or confusion, they don't need us to add to it. If you begin to bend or bail on your boundaries, you become just one more unpredictable factor in their life.

Life never actually slows down or settles—for any of us. Every day brings about a new change or challenge. But boundaries bring us and our relationships some security, predictability, and consistency. They are how we love our core values, ourselves, and others well—regardless of what life and the world might throw our way.

If you have a friend, coworker, or family member going through something challenging, they don't need inconsistency and unclear communication from you. They don't need you suddenly shrinking back, coddling their emotions, and watering down your words.

Everything in their life may be burning to the ground, and they may not have a clue what is coming next, but they will always find you unwavering, straightforward, and of sound mind. This is honesty. This is what you would want. This is what loving someone through pain looks like. You don't get swept away by their challenges or chaos; you stand firm in both grace and truth.

They don't need you to make things easier on them. They need you to be honest.

They don't need you to lessen their anxiety. They need you to be consistent.

They don't need you to fix their problems. They need you to hold the line.

They don't need you to cater to their feelings. They need you to remain confident.

When we care about others, we trust that, regardless of the

circumstances, healthy relationships always thrive off of healthy, consistent boundaries. We must remain committed to doing the right thing, even when it is hard, and especially when others don't entirely understand or like it.

RECURRING THEMES

I opened my computer, as I do most weekday mornings, to check my emails. One facet I love about working with women in my Discover Your Worth community is the email support I can provide. Here I am able to read their questions, give feedback, and witness their progress and personal breakthroughs.

I opened an email with the subject line, "Family boundary mess." I chuckled to myself, because, in the beginning, family and boundary work is almost always that—messy.

Lucy, a founding member of the DYW community, shared details of coming from a blended family—parents who divorced and then remarried new spouses, introducing stepsiblings into the mix. Her biological brother, whom she says she bonded with through the divorce, is struggling with addiction.

The problem Lucy wrote about centered on an upcoming family gathering, one that her brother would not be invited to due to his behavior. But here is what Lucy had the hardest time with: he didn't actually know he wasn't invited.

Lucy went on to share that not only did she feel as though they were all keeping this secret, but she also felt it was hypocrisy, as her stepsiblings were being treated with different level of tolerance by their parents. She grew guilty about attending the event herself, not wanting to abandon her brother or hurt him further. As I read on through the email, I began to look for the theme. Almost every email has one.

They start out as surface details, tit-for-tat exchanges between family members or friendship circles. But it became clear what the root issue was. This root issue would be important to identify so that healthy confrontation could be had to set a loving limit.

The first theme I noticed was that of loyalty. Since I had worked with Lucy for about a year, I had a good understanding of both her family of origin inventory and the core values she had identified prior.

It is always important that I remind my members what they value. For Lucy, we unpacked what it meant to be loyal. This isn't the same definition of loyalty she inherited from her family but instead was the new value she had written for herself since joining DYW.

I asked Lucy, "Does remaining loyal to your brother look like defending his poor choices made inside his addiction? Or is remaining loyal a reflection of loving him through allowing him to feel the pain of the consequences he receives based on his own behavior?"

Often, in the face of conflict, we can become confused and untethered to our new values and beliefs. The chaos on the outside can create chaos on the inside. Here we tend to bail on our progress, and ultimately our boundary practice, reverting to what is old and familiar, even if it is unhealthy. My job, then, is simply reminding women of their worth when they forget.

The second theme within the email I noticed was control. This is common with women who struggle with enmeshed family systems, especially since Lucy was used to playing the role of therapist, fixer, and rescuer. Again, it was important for me to remind her to take time to identify what her responsibilities were in this situation and, more importantly, what they *weren't*. While it is difficult to witness people we love engage in disagreement, it does not mean we must accept the invitation to step in and manage it. Part of learning how to engage in healthy conflict is learning how and when to disengage from conflict when it becomes unhealthy.

DISENGAGING FROM UNHEALTHY CONFLICT

Hopefully by now you are beginning to understand the importance of safe, healthy conflict, because as we've learned, *all conflict isn't created equal.* We need it, but we have to work to be intentional about engaging in the right kind of it—because of what it has the potential to produce. The right kind of conflict can be responsible for launching a successful new product with a coworker, problem-solving with a teammate on the playing field, growing closer to a friend or spouse, and communicating effectively with a teacher or peer in school. It is a skill we must pursue and practice.[2]

If healthy conflict wasn't modeled in your early relationships, then disagreements or debates can feel unsafe, even if you aren't a part of them directly. Due to this lack of safety, as in Lucy's case, it becomes tempting to try to control how other family members choose to interact with one another. You can't manage how others feel, think, or treat each other, but you can manage your response to it. This is done by growing intolerant to the unhealthy conflict and disengaging from it before it takes you down with it.

In Lucy's situation, she shared how she desperately wanted to manage how her brother felt about whether she decided to go to the family gathering. She was not able to tune in to what she needed and act accordingly, and instead began to base her decision on how he may act or feel if he found out she did go.

I encouraged her to remove

> **Part of learning how to engage in healthy conflict is learning how and when to disengage from conflict when it becomes unhealthy.**

her brother and the other family members from the equation for a moment. This is a helpful step when you want to get clear on the boundaries needed. I asked her a few questions: "If you decide to go to the gathering, will it derail your progress in any way? Will you feel safe while you are there? Will you feel tempted to manage or control the feelings in the room? Are you able to detach from the conflict happening between others? Can you enjoy yourself if you attend? Will you surrender the double standards and hypocrisy narrative as not yours to defend?" And perhaps most difficult: "Are you able to let go of managing how your brother feels or thinks about your decision?"

It took Lucy weeks to decide, and in the end, she did not go. Not because of what her brother needed but because of what she needed. She admitted that she simply wasn't ready, and going would cause her more harm than good. For the first time, she said, "I put a boundary on myself." That night, she honored herself and her decision by running a warm bath and reading a book in peace.

When we caught up later that week, I asked how she felt after not going. She shared that for a few days she worried she had missed out, but then she remembered that this was just the addiction to the chaos. She knew she didn't miss out on anything but arguing, gossiping, and negativity. She was proud of taking care of herself in ways that added to her continued healing, and a lot of that had to do with her personal responsibility in disengaging from the unhealthy conflict. She did what many have a hard time doing—she didn't just *do* better, she wanted to *become* better, and her choices reflected that.

We all have choices, and those choices will reflect how we will feel, where we will be, and whom we will be there with. Healthy relationships are built on and sustained through healthy conflict while knowing when to disengage if necessary.

ACKNOWLEDGE & CONFRONT

1. Have you ever avoided confronting a problem, only for that problem to later grow into something bigger? Explain.

2. How was conflict modeled to you growing up? Was it safe or unsafe?

3. Review the motives chart. Have you confronted someone recently and discovered your motive was unhealthy? Which unhealthy motive was it? And how did it go?

4. What roadblock have you experienced recently that distracted, derailed, or discouraged you from setting a healthy limit?

5. Have you ever tried to manage the conflict of others? How can you practice disengaging from unhealthy conflict in your relationships?

10

Boundaries in Action

HEALTHY BOUNDARIES ARE NOT WALLS KEEPING others out. I did not know this when I first began this practice, of course. When I discovered boundaries, I allowed the pendulum to swing a little too far. Let me explain.

My oldest daughter was in her second year of preschool. I walked her into her class as I did most mornings, unpacked her lunch box and water bottle into her cubby, then hung her backpack on the hook labeled with her name. I knelt down to give her a kiss goodbye and headed toward the door. Before I made it too far, I was stopped by her teacher.

"Mrs. Burg, did you get the email about our upcoming fall festival?"

"Yes, I did. Why do you ask?" I replied.

"Well, we need someone to help organize the activity booths. We were hoping you would volunteer to do that."

I felt myself immediately tense as my thoughts started to spiral. *I can't do any of that; I have a baby at home. I'm already so limited on time and energy. And I am not very craft-y or creative!* Before I knew it I had responded, "I am not able to do that this year, but I can ask Taylor's mom if she can."

I felt justified in my answer; after all, I was already spread thin at home. Later that month I would attend the fall festival with my daughter. There was a slew of activities for the kids to enjoy—a petting zoo, a face-painting booth, tractor rides, and even a pumpkin patch. But when I saw all the moms who had volunteered to help interact with the kids, I cringed. I knew in that moment I had missed an opportunity not only to serve my kid's school but to connect with other young moms. As I reflected, I thought I had been setting a boundary, and to some degree I was. But I didn't have the skill set to find flexibility in it, instead becoming too rigid based on my past commitments where my limits were nonexistent. Once again fear was in control, and I paid the cost.

Before we dive into what a healthy boundary is, it is important to first understand that boundaries live on a sliding scale, ranging from rigid to porous.[1]

| RIGID |————————————| HEALTHY |————————————| POROUS |

RIGID VERSUS POROUS

People with *rigid* boundaries desire to keep others at a distance. Here they can feel in control, and this control allows them to feel temporarily safe. They are highly independent. On the other hand, people with generally *porous* boundaries desire to keep others very close. Here they will overshare or get too involved in other people's lives. They are highly dependent.

Take note that your personal boundaries may be relative; you may have rigid boundaries with family but at work you have more porous boundaries or vice versa. This mix is common, but the goal is to work toward healthy boundaries no matter the setting or conditions.

RIGID	POROUS
Avoids being close in relationships out of fear of rejection or loss	Overshares personal information
Afraid to ask for help	Dependent on the opinions of others
Pretends not to care about what others think	Fears rejection and wants to be liked by everyone else
May come across as avoidant, cold, or detached	May come across as "go with the flow" or "easygoing"
Easily cuts off relationships	Accepts unhealthy behavior and treatment

HEALTHY BOUNDARIES

Healthy boundaries tend to be flexible in nature and fall somewhere within the rigid and porous range. They allow you to be seen, heard, and connected within your relationships because you are willing to get vulnerable. While rigid and porous boundaries are rooted in fear, healthy boundaries are not. When you are in a safe space, you don't overshare, because you are learning that this isn't being vulnerable—it's being impulsive and clingy. You don't overinvolve yourself in the lives, problems, and dramas of other people because you know you have your own priorities and responsibilities to care for.

Inversely, you don't undershare either; you allow others to get to know you gently, intimately, and, more importantly, wisely. You wait to discern if you can trust someone, and to what degree. You ask for help and allow yourself to lean on other people's strengths. It's this beautiful dance that is fluid and not forced.

If I better understood back then that all boundaries weren't created equal, I would have considered the sliding scale and not responded so impulsively to my daughter's preschool teacher. I had a bank of memories and moments when I'd said yes when I should have said no, and I feared living out more ugly ramifications, so I put up a wall.

I should have allowed myself a night or two to think it over before getting back to her with an answer. Hesitating is a powerful tool when setting healthy boundaries. Rushing to respond never makes for a flexible or creative alternative, and what I needed in this circumstance was a way to feel involved in some capacity without overextending myself. Knowing what I know now, I might respond today with something like, "I am not able to be the lead on organizing all the activities for the event, but I would be happy to sign up as a volunteer for one of the booths."

> **Hesitating is a powerful tool when setting healthy boundaries.**

It takes self-trust to call on boundaries that are flexible, a sort of trust that can feel distant or nonexistent if this is all new to you. Perhaps in the past, you walled people and experiences out, as I did. Or maybe you did the opposite and overcommitted. With time, you can learn to appreciate and use these former moments when you were too rigid or too porous as opportunities to adjust in the future.

Healthy boundaries

- stem from identifying and guarding your core values (which you have started identifying);
- are rooted in your core values, which aren't compromised based on other's opinions or expectations;
- allow you to be vulnerable safely and within the constraints of wise discernment (you do not over- or undershare);

- allow you to identify your personal needs and communicate them in a kind and clear way;
- allow you to say no and accept a no from others without offense;
- allow you to ask for help when it is needed, without being "needy"; and
- allow you to hear others' feedback with curiosity and openness.

Five signs you may have porous boundaries:

1. You don't speak up when someone treats you poorly.
2. You tend to feel tired, overwhelmed, and overscheduled.
3. You help someone out, then feel used by them.
4. You accept the blame for something that wasn't your fault.
5. You overshare about yourself without discernment.

Five signs you may have rigid boundaries:

1. You tend to keep relationships very "light," never getting too close.
2. You take others' feedback personally.
3. It is easy for you to cut someone out of your life.
4. Asking for help makes you feel "needy."
5. You rarely open up about yourself.

Remember, boundaries are on a sliding scale. They work for you; you don't work for them. At any one particular time, you can pause and decide whether a limit needs to be a bit firmer (rigid) or less firm (porous). Maybe if you are more rigid, start to notice when you need a little help and ask for it, or take a risk and share a small personal detail about yourself with someone safe. If you tend to be more porous, perhaps a good practice for you would be to restrain yourself from overcommitting or working to actively listen to someone else share.

When you try to make huge changes all at once, you are likely to quit right out of the gate. Instead, aim to take small steps in the most appropriate direction, depending on the relationship. Small and consistent changes are less dramatic and will allow you time to reassess according to your values, needs, and emotional safety at any given time. With practice, you will learn to trust your own judgment and gradually weave in healthier boundaries that will permeate all areas of your life. Oh—and don't worry about getting it perfect. In fact, stressing about perfection is a surefire way to stunt your progress. Instead, use your energy through practicing whenever possible. Role-playing is my favorite way.

Role-Play

We like to practice for everything. Think about it—we role-play for dance recitals, athletic games, and musical performances. An actor spends months, even years, rehearsing her part for a performance. Politicians and public figures practice their speeches out loud before ever setting foot behind a mic. When it comes to setting kind and clear limits, role-playing is the key to a confident delivery. Role-playing your boundaries may sound silly, but it ensures you find confidence in hearing yourself speak those limits first.

You may have discovered from the family of origin inventory you did earlier that you communicate the same way your earliest caregivers did. This might negatively affect your ability to clearly and kindly deliver a boundary today. Role-playing not only allows you an opportunity to grow confident in hearing something you've never heard yourself say out loud, but it also actively reinforces the new belief you have around no longer living loyal to a fault within your relationships.

Role-playing doesn't have to be a big production of you speaking your boundary statements out loud in front of your closest friends. It can be as simple as speaking the words out loud to yourself in the shower, in a mirror, or at every red light you hit while driving.

Let's walk through an example of this together.

Consider your kind, elderly neighbor named Mr. Bob. As sweet as he is, every time you check your mail, it seems he makes a beeline right for you to snag an *oh so veryyyyyy long* hug. It has gotten to the point where you wait until dark to check your mail or send your husband out to do it, which now feels ridiculous. You have decided that you are tired of walking on eggshells in your own driveway, so you begin to role-play out loud the limit you want to express to Bob. Role-play allows you to hear yourself say the boundary, so that when Mr. Bob swoops in, you are ready.

Every day while in the shower, for one whole week, you repeat to yourself out loud, "Mr. Bob, I don't want a hug today—how about a handshake?"

After one week, you feel ready. And, sure enough, here comes Mr. Bob. He's ready too. For his big ol' bear hug.

Your body language matches the limit you have practiced. Mail in one hand, you place the other hand up in a way that signals "stop."

You then proceed to say: "Hi, Mr. Bob, happy Monday. Today I don't want a hug. How about a handshake?"

To your surprise, Mr. Bob understands completely; he even apologizes for overstepping in the past. He says, "How rude of me . . . I never meant to make you feel uncomfortable."

"Thanks, Mr. Bob. How is your day going?" you ask. You chitchat briefly, then head back inside for the evening.

After setting your boundary, you no longer walk on eggshells in your own driveway. In fact, you now look forward to seeing Mr. Bob. During your small mailbox chats, you learn that he is a military veteran who had a daughter who would have been about your age now if she hadn't died of leukemia as a kid. Before, you would avoid Mr. Bob at all costs, but now you invite him over for dinner on Fridays. All this was made possible because of a boundary and two people's willingness to honor it.

While this may seem like an innocent and even trivial example, it isn't. I have hundreds of comments, emails, and messages that flood my inbox with everyday examples just like this. And after women choose to role-play and assertively communicate their limits, I have witnessed something cool happen. A different relationship can begin.

Minor Infractions

Minor infractions, like an unsettling hug from Mr. Bob, aren't as minor as we think. Women tell me all the time, "It wasn't that big of a deal" or "It seemed so small, I didn't want to bring it up." Yet they also reveal that their sleep, mood, and quality of life are all negatively affected by one minor infraction. We tell ourselves we can let it go, but we rarely ever do.

You don't have to wait for a big thing to happen to set a boundary and speak up. In fact, minor infractions are the perfect opportunity to role-play healthy confrontation. As Jen Wilkin writes, "What we repeat in times of ease, we will recall in times of hardship."[2]

We are well practiced at people-pleasing, at living overwhelmed, resentful, and bitter. Therefore, the only way to get better at setting appropriate boundaries is with practice.

Recall the previous section I wrote on resentment. Resentment isn't a result of one big thing. It's the culmination of a bunch of small things that, when left unaddressed, snowball into something more problematic. Setting boundaries helps eliminate resentment from our lives. Some opportunities to practice setting boundaries may seem trivial, but with practice, we can build confidence while getting rid of resentment.

I have a friend named Tracy who recently shared with me an issue she was facing at work. A female coworker of hers had casually mentioned that she once made out with Tracy's now husband (before my friend and her husband were married). Tracy explained that she froze up, as she was thrown completely off guard.

This is what can happen when we are not well practiced at boundary setting. Clearly, Tracy cares about her marriage. But because she had written off so many practice opportunities in the past as "small" or "minor," she lacked the confidence needed to draw a line with her coworker. Rather than kindly and clearly confronting her coworker about the inappropriateness of that comment, she defaulted to "playing it cool," and consuming this discomfort was costly. She suffered about a week of irritability, disappointment in herself, and tension within her marriage, admitting to arguing for days with her husband about it.

I am not saying what her coworker said was in some way Tracy's fault. I am saying it is our responsibility to prepare for moments like this. Practice with the little things, and the big things won't rock you so hard.

When you have clear limits and communicate them assertively, the discomfort falls back onto the person who has crossed the line. That can happen, of course, only if a line has been clearly drawn in the first place.

I encouraged Tracy to confront her coworker about the inappropriateness of that comment later (outside of work), when she felt less emotionally charged, and she did. While it didn't change what had happened, it did allow her to express that the comment was both hurtful and disrespectful, and that future comments like that would simply not be tolerated. It is never too late to do this, especially in an environment like work where she would encounter her coworker frequently.

Setting boundaries isn't without detours or potholes. You will trip up and you will fall short. Role-play allows you to practice solo with the small stuff, but it doesn't guarantee that it will always go smoothly. You may practice all day and night but, in a moment when you least expect it, freeze up or get tongue-tied, as Tracy did. But remember, progress is still progress, no matter how slow it is, and the discomfort of confronting someone imperfectly when they are out of line is far better than the suffering that ensues when you don't.

Deliver and Detach

You can identify your core values, monitor your healthy motives, and start role-playing to effectively communicate and deliver healthy, assertive boundaries. But there is another facet to this process that leaves many running for the hills: detaching from others' reactions.

When you begin setting healthy boundaries, you may become aware of others who have already been doing this work for themselves. Because of this, you can anticipate that when they hear your boundary, they will welcome it. This is in part because they are following the same set of "conflict rules" that involve confronting issues head-on in a safe and respectful way. They value you and the relationship, and they see the boundary as an opportunity for love, growth, or connection—*not as a personal attack*. They might not always agree with your limit, or entirely understand it, but they have a willingness to try to meet you halfway. This is what we hope for.

For some people, however, halfway is not an option. Regardless of how pure your motive is, or how kindly and clearly you deliver it, they will hear your boundary and it will result in a sudden and hurtful backlash. I want you to remember something: this is a result of their suffering, not your boundary.

If you encounter backlash due to setting a boundary, keep these few points in mind to help you detach:

- Avoid *explaining* the boundary. This reinforces your need to get your boundary approved by them. Explaining sounds like:

  "I can't help you move this weekend because my mother-in-law will be in town, and we have to take her to the doctor, then Sunday we have church and hopefully it won't rain so my daughter can go to the park with her friends. It's just a busy weekend and I really want to, but I just don't think we can do it . . . Is that okay?"

- Avoid *justifying* the boundary. This reinforces your need to get your boundary understood by them. Justifying sounds like:

  "I won't be able to let you pay your rent late again this month. I need that money because I am working to save for the down payment on a new car and I just had to pay for braces for Lacy and new baseball equipment for Luke."

- Avoid *apologizing* for the boundary. This reinforces your need to get your boundary accepted by them. Apologizing sounds like:

  "I am sorry, but I can't let you talk to me that way."

Their approval, understanding, and acceptance are out of your control. When you take your eyes off your limit and why you need what you do and turn outward toward their perception of your limit instead, you open up your boundary for negotiation. Not only that, but you are expressing your lack of confidence and uncertainty, leaving you vulnerable to their backlash tactics. This leaves the door open for anxiety, confusion, and bitterness to enter, and it's why many fall victim to bailing on their limits entirely. Remember, others will treat your boundaries how you treat your boundaries.

Backlash from a person you're setting a boundary with can be

Remember, others will treat your boundaries how you treat your boundaries.

vastly overwhelming. Terrifying even. Maybe you attempted to set a boundary in the past and have been on the receiving end of anger, passive aggressiveness, manipulation, pouting, threats, and more. Mistreatment like this may have you asking, *Why would any of this happen if boundaries are supposed to improve our relationships?* The truth is that boundaries often take away something that the other person is used to getting. This may be your time, your help, your money, your car, your attention, your advice, your approval, whatever it is. But I promise you, boundaries always give back to the relationship more than they take away. They change the dynamic of what has always been permissible, and for good reason. If the relationship can't handle your healthy boundary, then it may not be a relationship for you.

As you start setting boundaries and detaching from others' reactions to them, keep this verse close:

"Make up your mind not to worry beforehand how you will defend yourselves." (Luke 21:14)

It is understandable if you suddenly feel the urge to live on the defense, overly preparing yourself for any backlash that may come because of communicating a healthy limit. I want to encourage you that this is no way to be in a healthy relationship. It is possible to rest in your values, and although challenges will arise that are unpredictable, you can find peace in knowing that God will always equip you each step of the way.

BOUNDARY VIOLATIONS

As you embark on setting boundaries in your relationships, you will find that others will test your limits. Take for example my friend Katie, who called me when she was upset one afternoon.

"Court, you aren't going to believe what happened."

She then proceeded to tell me that just a week prior she'd attempted to set a boundary with her mother-in-law, who had a knack for bringing up Katie's weight whenever she was visiting. She decided, with her husband's support, to no longer let it slide.

After taking some time to role-play, she had given her mother-in-law a call to communicate her boundary, as they had plans to see her the following week. "I told her how excited I was to host her upcoming retirement party, but that when we are together, I can't allow her to talk about my weight anymore. I shared with her how it is both hurtful and embarrassing," Katie said.

Katie did the right thing. She had a clear motive: to spend quality time with her mother-in-law. She also predetermined and communicated what she would tolerate when they were together. These words were causing strain on their relationship, and pretending was no longer working.

Katie did her part, then went about planning the details for the retirement party. On the day of the celebration, Katie picked up the barbecue, wrapped the gift, and decorated the cake. Yet within minutes of guests arriving, her mother-in-law did in public what she swore in private she wouldn't do.

"Wow, Katie, looks like you haven't been working out as much as you said you have!" she exclaimed in front of old coworkers and unassuming family members.

"I was completely shocked," Katie said. "I felt so many things—hurt, angry, but mainly disappointed. I couldn't even enjoy the evening.

I kept replaying her words, over and over. I felt so uncomfortable in my own home and was counting down the minutes until everyone left so I could just cry."

I reminded Katie that this happens a lot when boundaries are a new practice, especially in families where they are otherwise nonexistent. And while Katie did her part up front, it would now be her responsibility to enforce the limit.

You may be wondering why Katie didn't say something in the moment, especially if she had been doing her practice of role-playing. In a situation like this, it can get sticky. Sometimes enforcing a boundary can and should be done in a group setting. At other times it is more appropriate to hold off until emotions aren't as charged and thinking is clearer. It is helpful to use wise discernment about when and how to approach healthy confrontation that may be necessary to uphold a limit you have previously set.

Katie, of course, admires her mother-in-law, but she later admitted that she was still a bit intimidated by her too. "When I am around her, I feel oddly like a little girl again. Her tone, body language, and backhanded comments make me feel so small."

Katie had to decide who she wanted to be in this relationship, and that would be determined by how she would respond to the clear boundary violation. Holding the line would allow her mother-in-law to be responsible for her own behavior so that Katie wouldn't have to be responsible for it anymore. It would also allow Katie to step into her rightful position as an adult woman who deserved respect too.

For days Katie wallowed in worry. And that's the hardest part of this whole process. We fear losing a connection, and we become highly focused on what *they* will say or do. It is helpful to remember in tense moments like this one that Katie and her mother-in-law weren't connecting very much before when her mother-in-law was criticizing Katie's weight. Instead, anxiety, bitterness, and anger were holding space where love could have been. Enforcing her healthy boundary gave the relationship a chance to thrive.

Katie now had two options.

She could choose to consume the discomfort and avoid confronting her mother-in-law, hoping the problem would resolve itself. Perhaps if she gave it some time, she would suddenly realize the weight of her words (pun intended). From my experience, women who choose this route tend to wait a *very, very long time.*

Or, Katie could confront her mother-in-law and the issue head-on. This may sound like, "I was so happy to celebrate you last week, but I want to talk about the comment you made about how much I work out and my weight. Again, that is extremely embarrassing and hurtful. I want to spend time together, but with comments like that, I simply can't."

This path allows Katie to reflect her motive again (to have quality time together) while also reiterating her primary boundary. She is also mindful of her tone—this serves to keep defenses down and allows a better shot at her boundary being heard.

Katie's response to her mother-in-law was a loving one. She wasn't being controlling, disrespectful, or overly sensitive, as some may assume. Instead, she was doing the messy work of enforcing a line she had drawn that was necessary for her to continue being in relationship with her mother-in-law. She was choosing to use boundaries because she cared about their relationship, not because she didn't.

BUMP UP THE BOUNDARY

When someone violates your boundary, as in Katie's situation, you always have options. In most cases a boundary violation requires you to do more than simply restate the boundary. Instead, you may need to "bump up" the boundary entirely. It is one thing to identify what boundary needs to be set, then to kindly and clearly communicate it. It is an entirely different beast to learn how to maintain it over time.

Unfortunately, many women fear boundary violations so much that they eventually abandon their boundary entirely (which is often a reflection of self-abandonment). Maintaining a boundary is a lot like teaching a young child to look both ways before crossing a road. You will have to remind her a lot. This isn't the same as justifying mistreatment. It is to say that a boundary practice is a skill that must be learned and maintained.

Upholding a healthy boundary won't happen by accident, and it won't be easy. You will have to sit through the discomfort of this process before you deem yourself worthy of healthy relationships that respect your limits. You will have to act in ways that honor who you are becoming long before you become her. It will require you to reinforce the boundary repeatedly when backlash arises or when violations increase.

Let's say Katie's mother-in-law, time and time again, violated her boundary and continued to make comments about Katie's weight. Katie then would have to decide whether she would continue believing her mother-in-law's promises to change or her behavior. From my experience, behavior is the more honest of the two. If she chose to believe her mother-in-law's behavior, bumping up the boundary would be her next option.

Options when your boundary is continually violated:

1. **Restate your boundary:** This is simply telling someone your original boundary again, with confidence, kindness, and clarity. For example, Katie would need to repeat, "I want to remind you, the next time I see you, to not make any comments about my weight."

2. **Create some space:** This can look like limiting your physical or verbal contact; perhaps you choose to no longer have playdates together, or you predetermine that you will spend time with this person only within the safety of a group setting. Katie choosing to remove herself from their family group-text chat would be an example of creating some healthy space.

3. **Take a break:** Here, you decide to take a break from interacting for a specific amount of time. For example, Katie might decide she will not invite her mother-in-law to the ladies' getaway she has planned for her birthday.

4. **Disconnect entirely:** This is exactly what it says. For Katie to continue becoming the best version of who she can be, she might need to decide to disconnect from the relationship permanently.

Sometimes bumping up the boundary even slightly is enough for the other person to feel the pain of their actions, and they do whatever it takes to change. This is the benefit of enforcing a *consequence* within the relationship. At other times, however, it may require more. With Katie, for example, her mother-in-law may not have taken her very seriously when she removed herself from the group chat, but missing out on spending time with her on Katie's birthday weekend may actually motivate change. Again, your bumping up the boundary isn't about controlling them. It's about taking responsibility for what you will tolerate and then managing the amount of access you allow those who violate your limits to have in your life.

Alternatively, many boundaries can offer up an *incentive*. Remember, boundaries are on a sliding scale and are not written in stone. Limits can be flexible and should work for you and your evolving relationships. Perhaps Katie's mother-in-law begins to refrain from talking about her weight, and over time Katie begins to trust her again. Her promises and words start to align; therefore, Katie may feel inclined to pursue more time together with her mother-in-law. This incentive can motivate Katie's mother-in-law to maintain her changed behavior, and the relationship can now develop at a healthy rate.

Unfortunately, not every relationship will result in changed behavior. Some relationships simply won't survive the process of you bumping up a boundary because it leaves the other person feeling attacked, controlled, or hurt. If this is the case, there is nothing you can do. Keep in mind, it is always a possibility that you will lose someone when you set or bump up a boundary, but you will eventually lose yourself if you don't.

It isn't easy stepping into your worth. In fact, it is costly. You will lose some people. You will anger and hurt some people. You will disappoint some people. But not setting boundaries is more costly. Many will settle for living their lives stressed, anxious, and unhappy, communing in relationships that reinforce and benefit from their lack of limitations. They become so afraid to rock the boat that they would much rather abandon themselves, their mental health, and their sanity just to keep the peace. Yet we simply can't serve the opinions and needs of others while also serving God (Luke 16:13).

We are conditioned through past generations to behave and respond in certain ways. Perhaps you were not equipped in how to begin or manage a boundary practice. And now that you are doing the work, it may feel at times that all this trying is draining. I am encouraged by what Craig Groeschel shares on this: "Trying is often an attempt to change with minimal commitment. Training is a whole-hearted commitment to achieve a specific result. When it comes to attacking our goals, being disciplined, or breaking bad habits, let's train our minds to stop trying and start training."[3]

The backlash and violations from others could cause you to revert to your old ways, but I pray that they don't. If you grow weary, it may help to shift your perspective from *trying* to *training*. Continue on, and trust that what is to come is far more valuable than anything you are leaving behind.

ACKNOWLEDGE & CONFRONT

1. Review the rigid-versus-porous chart. Which do you relate to more when it comes to setting boundaries?
2. Which direction on the scale (from rigid to porous) would your boundaries need to slide for them to become healthier? Explain.
3. Consider a time in the past when you let a "minor" infraction go. Did it eventually snowball into something bigger?
4. Think about a boundary that you need to set in a relationship right now. Write it down and identify when and how you will role-play it this week.
5. Have you ever bailed on your own boundary based on how other people reacted to it? If you could go back, would "bumping up the boundary" instead of bailing on it have better served the relationship long-term? Explain.

11

The Loop Around

A FEW YEARS INTO USING BOUNDARIES IN MY relationships, I decided to begin seeing a therapist whose name was John. I sat across from him every week on Mondays at 10:00 a.m. He sat on a swivel chair; I sat on an ugly, green couch. I would stare out the window just over his right shoulder, trying to gather my thoughts. I often felt unsure of what we would talk about and began to wonder if that window was for other uncertain people like me to look out of.

"How are things?" he asked.

"Fine," I replied.

Every week it would start off like this. Slow. Subtle. And he would wait.

Finally, I said, "She texted me last night."

"Who?" he asked.

"My mom."

"Oh, what did she text?"

"She said my brother just went to jail. He was reported by DCF [Florida Department of Children and Families] again, so they locked him up."

"I see. How did that make you feel?" he asked.

"Scared. Sad. Angry. *Everything*," I replied.

"Well, did you respond?" he asked.

"No, I didn't. I wanted to. But I knew not to trust my first response."

"What would that have been, Courtney?"

"It would have been to pry. Get more info. I want to know what happened. Who has my nephew now? How would my brother find money for bail? What could I do to help?"

John then pulled out a piece of paper. "Have you ever seen this before?" he asked, drawing a triangle on the page. "This one corner is where the victim lives. And over here in this other corner is the persecutor. And finally, this corner . . . the rescuer. Right now, that's you." He was illustrating to me what is known as the Karpman drama triangle.

- *Victims* act helpless and incompetent. They may feel they have done all they can do to fix a situation, yet avoid responsibility and depend on the rescuer.
- *Rescuers* act as enablers of the victim, taking on the victim's responsibilities and avoiding their own.
- *Persecutors* act as blamers and are often critical and judgmental of both the victim and the rescuer.[1]

Over the next few sessions John helped me better understand that my brother was capable of helping himself but was choosing not to. He also pointed out how the urge I felt to dig for more information was an old pattern of behavior that helped me feel connected. While it seemed harmless, I was accepting an invite to join in on the chaos.

I learned that the drama triangle was like a game in which each player feeds off and into the next, causing continued suffering and misery for all. The roles are interchangeable, depending on context, of course.

I was playing the rescuer when I bailed my brother out of jail or paid his rent.

I was playing the victim when I blamed my family for taking my help, even though I kept offering it.

I was playing the persecutor when I judged or criticized my parents for enabling his behavior.

This new knowledge left me completely floored. I knew at times I felt like I had to rescue others, but I never considered how at times I also played the other roles. I began to see how I lacked personal responsibility, and this left me stuck repeating the same patterns of unhealthy behavior.

It took time to implement what I had just learned, and once I did, I found myself a bit jaded. Days without the drama I was used to suddenly felt dull and eerily quiet. I would like to share that I had this profound experience where my tendency to involve myself in the drama triangle suddenly dissipated. It didn't. I did, however, choose to lean into my relationship with God. You see, whenever I feel completely rescued by Jesus, I no longer desire to rescue others, as I know my way of rescuing will never compare.

> **Whenever I feel completely rescued by Jesus, I no longer desire to rescue others, as I know my way of rescuing will never compare.**

I would also have to decide over and over again that the way to end playing the game for myself would be to simply quit playing it.

I wrote on my vanity mirror these reminders:

I can be mindful of my energy.
I can mind my own business.
I can be a responsible adult.

I can be right where my feet are.

I can send the call to voice mail.

I can love them and still say no.

I can quit playing the drama game.

Each time I was invited into the "triangle," I had to fight off the temptation to join in. As much as I wanted to connect, know more, and offer up solutions or help, I reminded myself that in this sort of game, no one actually wins. In fact, healthy relationships are void of games entirely.

At times I would have to be direct, when ignoring or disengaging from the drama wasn't enough. This would sound like, "That's none of my business" or "I don't want to talk about him with you." And I would almost always have to learn how to sit in the discomfort of life being less chaotic. I would eventually learn to enjoy a pace that was both peaceful and predictable. While for a long time this felt artificial and uncomfortable, it slowly became my new norm.

THE LOOP AROUND

I came up with the phrase "avoiding the loop around" as a mental reminder of the urge one can feel when one sets a boundary and desperately wants to go back on it. It is what happens when the old tapes begin to play, and you begin to lose access to your sound mind. Often the loop around is fueled by flooding emotions, fears, panic, and regret.

The loop around is what happens when you attempt to replant what God had pruned.

Take for example the previously mentioned text from my mother about my brother. I had already resigned myself to no longer managing the trouble my brother was in. In the past I would have offered bail money, driven to help with my nephew, or, at the very least, become a sounding board for my parents to vent their concerns and complaints. But not anymore. I had made my limits clear, and I would stand firm in maintaining them.

Knowing how to assert my limits didn't mean I didn't still want to do all of these things. Clearly, as I sat in John's office, I was battling the temptation. I still longed to return to the people, places, and behaviors that once served me but no longer did. I wanted to know the details and how I could help, and more than anything else, I wanted to be connected. But connection through chaos is never actually connection.

When I am tempted by the loop around, I notice it always accompanies a bit of a panic within. I share a limit and I feel a sudden urge to go back on it—fast. I know it is unhealthy and an old default pattern because it usually involves some sort of attempt at making things feel or appear better.

A loop around may look like:

Texting to make sure they aren't mad at me.
Gifting them things or words to earn their adoration again.
Going back on my limit because I can't handle being alone.
Contorting myself so I can fit in and feel worthy.

Yet I can notice this urge to loop back around and decide. I can choose whether I will believe the old lies that kept me returning to unhealthy patterns, working for love and acceptance, or I can trust that God has more in store for me, even when I can't see what that is. I can turn to a safe friend, a certified therapist—heck, even a workout or a new book—to help me resist and process.

Maybe, for where you are right now, you are doing the work to establish boundaries in your relationships and some people don't like it. Maybe you feel the urge to loop back around, and this is influenced greatly by the pressure you feel from outsiders. These people, the ones indirectly related to your boundary, are who I call the spectators.

SPECTATORS

Spectators are the people who have a more challenging time with your boundary than the person or people the boundary is specifically for.

Take for example setting a healthy boundary with your parents. You share with them that you won't be able to make it to Easter weekend at their house because you will be out of town visiting your husband's parents that weekend. All seems well, until you get a call from your sister. She heard about your plans and doesn't understand. She even sounds a bit upset by it all. She wants you to explain and then call your mother back and apologize because, she says, "Mom is so unsettled and hurt." Your sister is now acting as the spectator.

Remember, you have previously decided you are no longer going to be pulled back into managing the feelings of others. And while her call has you bubbling up with feelings of your own now, you exercise self-control by not bending on your boundary, or spending any precious energy attempting to manage what her or your mother have to say or think about it.

In a situation like this you will experience the upset that accompanies disrupting the way "things have always been." Perhaps you are the first person to begin setting boundaries, and that stings for all involved. In the past you may have allowed a call from your sister to change your plans. You might have even lost sleep over the idea of hurting your mother. But now you see the value of a healthy boundary practice.

The spectators tend to think of themselves as peacemakers. They find the disruption so uncomfortable that they launch into referee or mediator role, working to fix the disruption and ease the discomfort *fast!* Spectators usually mean well, but by inserting themselves into a problem that isn't theirs to solve, they tend to add more noise and chaos to the situation at hand. I have found that the disruption reminds them of their own inabilities to set and maintain a boundary. They may even become a bit jealous of your newfound freedom.

While it can be challenging, it may help to remind yourself that spectators crave boundaries but aren't sure how to use them at first. This was once you. It takes time to break free from old patterns that hold us captive. Maintaining this perspective may create some compassion and allow you to detach with love when necessary.

Remember, you can set and maintain a boundary even when others don't like or agree with it. Let everyone feel what they need to, without making it your responsibility to manage. Upset and confused feelings are a part of the change for everyone. Change causes movement, and movement causes friction.

REWIRING

When you begin to set and maintain healthy boundaries, old tapes of thinking will begin to play in your mind. These are part of your brain's wiring, prompting you to do what you have always done, on autopilot of sorts. Your brain wants to preserve resources, and so it will resist change.

The good news is, your sound mind can literally change how your brain functions. This is the power of neuroplasticity. Simply put, you can become more resilient in your relationships by thinking differently.

I especially respect the work of Dr. Caroline Leaf in this field.

Her research highlights just how powerful our minds are and how we can change what we do simply by how we respond in challenging moments. She shares three ways to develop your mental resilience and change your brain:

- When you find yourself feeling hopeless, stop and tell yourself that your brain can change. Tell yourself that your brain is plastic, and you can use your thinking to change your mind and take control of your life. Write down your thoughts if you find that this will be helpful. Practice doing this for 3 weeks (it takes 21 days to *start* changing neural pathways).
- Over the next 21 days, pay attention to what other people say to you. If it is negative, do not meditate on their words. Forgive them, and fight the desire to take any negative comments into your mind. Remember, whatever you think about the most grows, affecting your ability to think, speak and act.
- Spend a few moments every day for the next three weeks focusing on challenges you have overcome in the past. Remind yourself of your strength and ability to not only survive but also thrive.[2]

Remember in an earlier chapter when we unpacked how to think about our thoughts? This is crucial, because God wants you to be sound in both mind and body (2 Tim. 1:7).

Beliefs/values → thoughts → actions

If we want to change how we act, we must work to change how we think. This takes awareness and doing things differently, even when it is uncomfortable. You will use mental energy to change your patterns of behavior, until those patterns are no longer new. Instead they become what you know (default).

For example, it may be difficult to navigate the incoming calls from your sister about your plans for Easter; after all, she is persistent. Her voice mails include comments about your selfishness and demand an explanation. The thoughts in your head begin to race, oscillating between *Maybe I am selfish . . . ?* and *Is this really such a big deal?* She *is* your sister, and this is hard because it is the first time you are going against what everyone wants and expects from you. But you can choose to notice these thoughts and feelings and not allow them to dictate your next move.

RECLAIM A SOUND MIND

You have a sound mind, given to you by God as a tool to decide what you want to do with your thoughts and feelings at any given time. But the Enemy wants you to choose to act *before* you think, or at the very least, he will encourage you to choose to act based on *how you think*. We have to combat this by keeping our thoughts in Christ.

Thoughts and feelings are not bad, but what we choose to do with those thoughts and feelings can be destructive or counterproductive. With a sound mind you can begin to act in ways that reinforce your core values and boundaries and, above all, honor God.

Pull out a notepad and do this quick exercise.

You see how this works? You write down what you are thinking and feeling in the moment. This helps you acknowledge the powerful energy that is swirling around in your head and heart. You then hold them up to the Father, asking for his feedback on them. You essentially say, "Hey, Dad, what do you think about these?"

In Greek, "sound mind" is *sózó*, "to be saved or delivered," and *phrén*, "one's mental inclination or pattern of thought."[3]

So a "sound mind" quite literally means to be saved from our own mental inclination. Thank you, Lord.

WHAT AM I THINKING/FEELING?	HOW DO THESE HOLD UP TO SCRIPTURE?
I feel bad for setting this limit.	"Therefore, there is now no condemnation for those who are in Christ Jesus." (Rom. 8:1)
I am overwhelmed by all the things I feel I am responsible for.	"Come to Me, all you who labor and are heavy laden, and I will give you rest. Take My yoke upon you and learn from Me, for I am gentle and lowly in heart, and you will find rest for your souls. For My yoke is easy and My burden is light." (Matt. 11:28–30 NKJV)
I have anxiety about what my other family members will think.	"Do not be anxious about anything, but in every situation, by prayer and petition, with thanksgiving, present your requests to God." (Phil. 4:6)

When you compare your thoughts and feelings to Scripture, you not only engage in intimate communion with God but you begin the practice of claiming authority over your thoughts and rewiring your thinking. When you get clear on what you think, and you choose to act only on true thoughts, your behavior benefits.

This simple yet efficient exercise is one you can do at any time. You can do it sitting at the beach. You can do it waiting in a car line. You can do it while getting groceries. At any moment you can analyze your own thinking and feeling and test it against Scripture. "When we declare God's truths over our lives, we are not denying negative facts or circumstances. Rather, we're choosing to focus on the higher reality of God's truth."[4] You always have access to a sound mind. What a gift.

You may at times feel guilty for caring for yourself. But remember, this is a part of your old default patterns. Like crabs in a bucket trying to climb their way out, instead of encouraging each other toward freedom, they grab onto others and subsequently pull them (and themselves) back down. Yes, they are together, and maybe this brings some comfort. But that's where they spend the rest of their days, in the bucket. Stuck. Until they all die.[5]

His way is *the way*. It is the truth and the life (John 14:6). Cling to his Word, because you can trust it is always true—yesterday, today, and tomorrow (Heb. 13:8). Remind yourself you are allowed to climb out of that bucket, no matter who decides to come with you. It isn't your fault or responsibility if they choose to stay. What a privilege it is to access the power of a sound mind.

ACKNOWLEDGE & CONFRONT

1. Consider the Karpman drama triangle. Are you able to identify when you play the rescuer, persecutor, or victim in your relationships? How might a boundary on yourself allow you to quit playing the game? Explain.

2. Have you been tempted to "loop around" after setting a boundary? Describe that situation.

3. Do you have a "spectator" in your life who intervenes whenever you try to set a boundary? Have *you* ever been a spectator trying to keep the peace in other people's relationships?

4. When is the last time you acted before thinking? How did that turn out?

5. Take some time to work through the thinking/feeling exercise to compare to Scripture a current thought or feeling you are carrying today. Is it true according to God's Word?

12

Safe Versus Unsafe People

MY SON JUST TURNED TWO, AND HE IS OBSESSED with anything on wheels. Papa's red truck. Motorcycles. Semis. Big diggers. We even watch the same YouTube video of "Wheels on the Bus" on repeat. And if we aren't busy doing that, he can be found racing through the house zooooooming by like Lightning McQueen, usually naked (all boy moms know what I am talking about).

Now, like my son, I want you to imagine you are on a racetrack. (It is up to you whether or not you have clothes on.) This racetrack is the track of life. Let's allow some NASCAR terminology to help us remember the influence others can have on our journey.

On this racetrack of life there are a bunch of other cars. They go fast. Some drivers drive well. Others don't. And then there is you, trying to figure out how to stay safe and in your lane. NASCAR slang for this is "the groove." It's the best route around the track and can depend on many conditions. Finding your groove is like learning how to spot the red flags of unsafe people, or knowing when and how to welcome the comfort of safe ones.

As you begin to take some laps around the track, you realize you need to set boundaries with the unsafe people in your life, and you also should begin to set some healthy boundaries with yourself. You pick up speed, and as you do, you begin to feel resistance. This is what is considered "the drag," and it's due to a change in speed and direction. You can expect that others will not always like, approve of, or support the new work you are doing, but you can continue down your new path *regardless*.

Then, suddenly, you find yourself "side drafting" due to the airflow disruption of other cars bumping by. You get distracted and lose some momentum. Perhaps you allow a spectator to dump some of their fears, doubts, or concerns on you. Or maybe you get a little off track because of a roadblock statement or a yellow caution flag. You remind yourself that you have to stay focused, eyes on the finish line. This is Talladega Superspeedway, after all.

Some of the other cars become difficult to pass. You experience some turbulence and rough patches. You notice that for a few laps you have trusted some unsafe cars, all of which has left you dealing with the wake of "dirty air." You even find moments when you may lose control, but you don't let this stop you. You remember you can regroup at any time, and you do, realigning yourself with the next safe car you see, and you keep going. *Hands on the wheel.*

You begin to find more safe cars, ones that aren't distracting or discouraging. The drivers aren't looking at the spectators, as they are focused on their own race. They are staying in their lane and picking up speed, and as you near them, this momentum allows you to do the same. You feel more at ease, and your grip on the wheel loosens. They are showing you the way, maybe because they have driven this road before, or maybe because they see the same finish line you do. Their wake of air is turbulent, powerful, and "clean," allowing you to drive with ease and confidence. Together your high speeds and power create a "down force," planting the car firmly on the ground, undisturbed and able to do what it needs to. *These are your safe people.*

Before you know it, you see the checkered flags waving. You begin "drafting," catching a boost of speed just as you cross the finish line. You did it, and you did it well.[1]

SAFE PEOPLE

Now, I know you didn't plan to get a lesson in NASCAR, but my hope is to get you thinking a bit more about the power of influence. You quite literally are headed where those around you are headed. It is always possible to be thrown into a tailspin by the beliefs, words, and behavior of people who choose to disown their unsafe traits. You can expect some resistance when you begin, but this resistance can't be the reason you lose sight of where you are headed. Developing safe relationships will ensure that you get to the finish line with speed, confidence, and power.

We have covered the many important benefits of healthy boundaries. They allow you to feel safe, to guard your core values, to know others, and to be known by others through authentic connection. I mentioned in an earlier chapter that part of this would be determined by practicing healthy confrontation within the constraints of safe relationships. Knowing how to determine who is safe and who is unsafe will be best done through wise discernment.

As you embark on setting healthy boundaries, you may find that many of your close relationships do not feel safe. Some of them may be doused in recurring drama or generated chaos. Conflict in these relationships seems to swing between some form of overreactivity or underreactivity (both of which are harmful). You may even begin to discover that you are not very safe yourself, and you now want to change that.

Imagine a clean cloth and a dirty cloth. If you rub a perfectly spotless clean cloth together with a dirty, oily, smudged cloth, what happens? The dirty cloth will make the clean cloth dirty too. The condition of each cloth is dependent not on how pristine the clean cloth is but rather on the condition of the dirty one.

The same can be said for our relationships. We want to believe that if we stick around longer, if we do more or work harder, if we try to stay superclean, we will eventually rub off on those around us. And to some degree, we may. But more times than not, you will be far more influenced and affected by the negative behavior and unsafe traits of others first. It's why it can be tempting to gossip, complain, or lie when others around you do.

If you can stay brutally honest with yourself, which is highly important in this work, you will learn that returning to unsafe relationships is very self-serving. While you may give a lot in your unsafe relationships, and lose a lot in the process, you also gain something too. It's called a payoff.

Take for example a member in my DYW community named Pamela. Time and time again, she found herself dating what she would call the "needy" type. Initially, she liked that these men were sensitive and open with their feelings. She even appreciated their willingness to share about their challenges so candidly. But over time the same thing would happen. She would begin to do most of the emotional lifting in the relationship and would start to resent that she never felt cared for or tended to. On dates she would hear herself offering up advice or suggestions, until one day she made a breakthrough. Pamela finally realized that while she knew deep down that she didn't see these guys as long-term partners, she did like being needed. This payoff was how it was serving *her*. And while all these men were generally kind and polite, the payoff would not be enough to establish and maintain the healthy, safe relationship she desired.

After reviewing her family of origin inventory and working to uproot some limiting beliefs, Pamela realized that her father had relied on her a lot for emotional stability. He would complain about work and his health, and at times he would even need rides to work or to borrow rent money. She liked being needed by him because this was how she maintained their connection. She feared that if she stopped being helpful, he wouldn't need her anymore, and without being needed, she would lose this connection and, ultimately, his love. She ended up carrying this belief and pattern of behavior into her dating life.

Pamela chose to take accountability for the part she was playing in returning to relationships that once served this short-term payoff and began to consider what she wanted in a relationship long-term. She began challenging the limiting belief she carried around about earning a man's love in the same way she had earned her father's love, and she started to see the unsafe traits in her suitors as exactly what they were: *unsafe*. This, of course, meant that Pamela had to work to become the type of safe person she hoped to attract one day. And in moments when she felt drawn back to her old patterns, she knew that setting a healthy boundary for herself would be necessary. Pamela no longer found unsafe relationships attractive, which over time was reflected in how she carried and cared for herself in the dating world.

UNSAFE VERSUS SAFE

Unsafe qualities may be present in a relationship if:

- They withdraw when you tell them no.
- They don't encourage you to do things without them.
- They use guilt or manipulation to get their way.
- They act like you are responsible for their feelings.

- They are highly attuned to your faults yet unaware of their own.
- They are confusing, unreliable, and attracted to drama.

Safe qualities may be present in a relationship if:

- They respect your boundaries.
- They are trustworthy and honest.
- They are encouraging and supportive.
- They use the same "rule book" of healthy confrontation.
- They are clear, consistent, and reliable.
- They don't find chaos or drama attractive.

Beth Moore reminds us, in her study of Isaiah called *Breaking Free*, that unsafe people are instantly intimate and increasingly controlling. Unsafe traits aren't reason enough to throw in the towel every time, as we are all human and fall short of the glory of God (Rom. 3:23). Unsafe traits are, however, something we must pay attention to.

Often, unsafe traits are habitual in nature—automatic and unconscious. They are so deeply woven into some people's identity that often they won't notice they are even doing them. Your early caregiver might have used lying or manipulation to secure control. Your spouse finds making passive-aggressive comments an easy alternative to releasing underlying anger or disappointment. A coworker prefers to shame you for your flaws rather than build you up through your weaknesses. A friend disappears when challenges arise between you because confrontation scares her. These unconscious or automatic tendencies can become the "normal" in our relationships, destroying us and our relationships if we let them.

I didn't want to admit that I was unsafe. Yet when I discovered the book *Safe People* by Dr. Henry Cloud, I began to see just how dysfunctional my patterns of behavior had become. One situation was a friendship I allowed to get too serious, too quickly.

Holly and I had just met through a mutual friend. She was tall, blond, and very successful in her career. I admired the way she dressed: business casual, unlike me in my everyday uniform of yoga pants and tank top. She had a confidence about her that was appealing and a smile that was deeply contagious. I immediately liked her and wanted to be her friend.

The weeks that followed were sort of a whirlwind. We talked about everything from our marriages to our parents to the trouble we got into back in high school. I found myself telling her things I hadn't told many people. Then suddenly I stopped hearing from her. I began to panic, as a rush of thoughts flooded in. *Did I overdo it? I thought we were besties. What happened?*

I did overdo it, but that's not what happened to Holly. She had the flu and, a few weeks later, would be transferred to another state for work. Needless to say, we weren't besties despite the fact that I had convinced myself we were. I ran into our mutual friend some months later, only to hear about myself—Holly had told her the intimate details of our private talks. Holly was not only untrustworthy but she had a history of having many "best friends." I have since learned if you are best friends with everyone, you're not best friends with anyone.

That's when I began to spot the red flags, not just in others but in myself too.

RED FLAGS

Red flags are little warning signs to be aware of in existing relationships, or within new ones, like with Holly and me. Knowing these will allow you to begin taking ownership over your own unsafe traits and decide at which pace and to what depth you will go in your relationships. Red flags include the following:

- **It's moving too quickly.** Unsafe relationships dive in headfirst, where too much is exchanged too soon.
- **You fear losing each other.** When fear is in control, you cling to some pattern of behavior that is unhealthy. Jealousy is present, as are insecurity, anxiety, and doubt.
- **You crave controlling them or being controlled by them.** There is a constant lack of personal responsibility because boundaries are blurred.
- **You are caught up in the drama triangle.** The rescuer, victim, and persecutor roles are commonly played.
- **You are unable to manage conflict in a productive and healthy way.** Issues are blown out of proportion or ignored entirely.

More times than not, I see women running toward unsafe people, accepting others' lack of ownership as an invitation to step in and do their work for them. Or they deny or excuse their unsafe qualities. This simply perpetuates the cycle and reinforces the behavior, and it's why many live stuck, exhausted, bitter, and unsatisfied in their relationships. But there's a better way. When a relationship isn't working, we can run to God for his thoughts on why—and trust him with the answers.

There are many more red flags to look for, but this will get you started. Again, unsafe traits aren't reasons to not be in relationship with someone, as only one perfect man has ever walked this earth. But we can train ourselves in discernment and begin exercising self-restraint. As you work to become a safer person, your relationships will reflect it.

LITMUS TEST

If we are all unsafe to some degree because of our humanness, then how do we know when to stick around and when not to? Well, I have found there is one key component that makes all the difference: *willingness*. If someone carries unsafe traits yet shows the willingness to move toward safety in their relationship with you, then that relationship is worth the continued effort.

Brené Brown describes vulnerability as using courage for "uncertainty, risk, and emotional exposure." It's that unsure feeling we get when we don't have control as we step outside our comfort zone.[2]

That's what this process is—stepping outside your comfort zone. When you are in control, you rarely take risks. But risk-taking will be necessary to connect deeply with others. When you remember God is in control, you can pursue meaningful relationships without fear. Risk-taking is done best within the healthy constraints of wise discernment.

Discernment isn't the same as judging or being highly critical of others. It is easy to distance yourself from people and call this "discernment" when it's really you not wanting to relinquish control or take a risk. Using what I call the *litmus test* in your relationships will help you develop wise discernment and know what relationships are worth your energy and time.

If you aren't familiar, litmus tests date back to the early 1900s and were used by scientists to determine which compounds were more acidic or alkaline in nature.[3] It was a simple test in which a drop of the sample compound was applied to the colored litmus paper. Based on what color the paper turned, the scientists could better identify its pH level.

We can use this idea of a litmus test to learn how to navigate new or existing relationships with better discernment. These tests allow you to pause and consider the relationships you are in from a rational, wise standpoint. You see, when you are in the early stages of learning new patterns of behavior, often you can't (and shouldn't) trust your knee-jerk reactions. These tend to be survival skills and coping mechanisms that you no longer need. The litmus test allows you to analyze the true character of someone based on their behavior, words, and actions. Again, when someone shows us who they are, we have to believe them.

An easy way to apply the litmus test to your relationships moving forward is to ask yourself:

In what ways are they influencing me?
How do their priorities differ from mine?
To what degree do our values align?
Are they willing to work on their unsafe traits?

Take for example my friend Bethany. For years Bethany and I were very close. But when I began uprooting the old limiting beliefs I carried about my friendships and started identifying my core values, I realized promptness was important to me. It was a quality I wanted in my close friendships that exhibited both good stewardship and mutual respect.

Bethany, however, did not value being on time like I did. She valued lots of other wonderful things, but promptness she did not. Try as she may, she will one day be late for her own funeral. This doesn't make Bethany a bad friend. It simply means we value different things, and knowing this allowed me to reevaluate the amount of energy I poured into the friendship. We can choose to stay in relationship with others who have different values from ours. But we should consider the amount of energy, time, and priority we are placing on those relationships.

I was also able to adjust what I could control, which was how often we got together. Before, we would get together several times a month. I would wait on her for lunch, staring at my watch as my irritation grew and grew. And by the time she did arrive (sometimes up to forty minutes late), I really wasn't in the mood to chat anymore. I would leave in a rush, after scarfing down my food, only to internally blame her for my feeling frenzied the rest of the day.

I no longer do this to myself or to Bethany. I began asking myself those same hard questions around values, influence, and priorities. I also started taking responsibility for what I was allowing and for how this allowance was affecting me and our friendship. Now, I meet with Bethany less frequently, and I make sure I don't have anything scheduled right after. I also order my meal at the time we decided to meet (and not when she arrives late) so that I can enjoy my lunch without rushing. And if we have only an hour together planned, then I excuse myself when that hour is up without guilt or annoyance. I am now better able to love Bethany for who she is, not for who I expect her to be.

I didn't communicate any of this to Bethany, however, because I didn't have to for it to still benefit our friendship. Sometimes a boundary is nonverbal and internal, involving small choices that you commit only yourself to. I won't be able to change what Bethany values, but that doesn't mean I have to bend on what I value either. Instead, I can decide not to blame her for why our lunch dates left my afternoons a hot mess. Before Bethany's behavior would offend me, but now I know it isn't personal. And although this one value was different, most of our friendship is incredibly enriching.

Alternatively, sometimes differing values will leave you

> Sometimes a boundary is nonverbal and internal, involving small choices that you commit only yourself to.

less accommodating. Consider this example: You are in a season of stewarding your finances to build a new home one day, and saving is a value that you have acquired to meet this goal. (Remember, values help drive your mission.) Yet you have this one close friend who simply doesn't get it. She invites you to attend dinners, get pedicures, or go shopping. The value of saving is not on her agenda, and to some degree, neither is your continued friendship. Again, this doesn't make her wrong. It just means your values aren't aligned in this season. The litmus test allows you to test, review, and analyze to ensure you don't get discouraged or distracted. Perhaps she can remain a good friend but not a close one, and that's okay. This acceptance does two things: it allows you to love her for who she is, void of bitterness and blame, and it allows you to maintain your progress toward building that home.

The litmus test allows you continued self-inventory and responsibility. When you observe the patterns of behavior that others are generally accustomed to, you no longer expect for them to suddenly be who they are not. In the same regard, you do not have to live with the constant pressure of morphing into what they need you to be to stay in close relationship. It's no longer a tug-of-war but rather an empowered commitment to both acceptance and action. Here, you begin to take wise steps toward healthy discernment while also rebuilding your self-trust in the process.

ACKNOWLEDGE & CONFRONT

1. Review the list of unsafe traits. Identify the area(s) you need to work on to become safer.
2. Have you spotted a red flag in a relationship before and chose to ignore it? How did that turn out?
3. Have you ever had a relationship that went too fast, too soon? Explain.
4. Consider your closest three relationships and work through the litmus test questions. Reflect on what you discover.
5. When people show you who they are, do you believe them? Or do you manufacture or justify a new version of them that keeps you returning to the relationship? Explain.

PART 3

Legacy Writing

IN PART 1, I HOPE YOU TOOK SOME TIME TO WORK through the family of origin (FOO) inventory and started to become more aware of the unhealthy relational patterns you inherited in childhood. Perhaps you have even started identifying your own core values and are taking small steps toward guarding them with healthy boundaries.

In part 2, I offered practical solutions, which are tools you can return to at any time for both reminders and encouragement.

Now, in part 3, I hope to highlight how this work affects your power of influence and legacy. Setting boundaries in your relationships requires taking continued personal responsibility, which will benefit not only your current relationships but the relationships that will exist once you are gone.

It is not lost on me how difficult this work can be. At times it can feel very lonely. There will be certain relationships in this life that will never be restored, no matter how much effort you put in. You can grieve, question, and wrestle with this and with God, which can be an important part of the process. You may also find a season where he is asking you to go without for a while.

Without old relationships.

Without your old patterns of behavior.

Without any answers.

Yet stay encouraged. In my experience, I have found that those seasons of going *without* are necessary for a transformation to happen *within*.

13

Friendship

I WAS DOING ALL THE WORK TO HEAL FROM codependency and was getting better at setting and maintaining healthy boundaries with myself and in my relationships. Yet God began to reveal an area that I was still hesitant to work on: friendships with other women.

I didn't know a thing about being a good friend. For years I knew only how to be an unhealthy friend. I knew how to say yes and show up to help a girlfriend out, only to spread myself too thin again and resent her for it later. I knew how to contort myself into what a girlfriend wanted me to be just so that I could ensure I would be included. I knew how to take a girlfriend under my wing as a personal project I believed I could fix, or how to compete with or compare myself to her. I knew how to criticize and judge her behind her back but still somehow manage to fake it to her face to ensure I always made it on a photo square within her perfectly curated social media feed.

I never allowed any girlfriend of mine to get too close. I had a long, strained relationship with my own mother and had no sisters, which didn't help set me up for success with other women. I had also been burned in the past with girlfriends, and I'd be lying if I didn't say I still held on to some of that residue. While I had forgiven my mother and these other women as well as myself, I still lacked trust, which often is what kept my friendships surface level and sporadic. I would live timid and just distant enough so that when things slightly began to sour, get hard, or turn weird, I could easily pull away. No harm done. *Or so I thought.*

SHARING BURDENS

I met Crystal at a playdate; her son was the same age as my oldest daughter. You can probably picture it if you have ever had small children: squeaky toys, crawling kids, and snack crumbs scattered about—plus a few tired moms mingling close by trying to exchange some easy conversation amid the noise.

Crystal and I immediately hit it off, and while I felt connected on many intimate levels, I never allowed her to get too close. Our friendship continued over the years until suddenly I heard that her mother was battling cancer.

I checked in without letting my guard down, which usually meant through text. Some days she would reply and send me a picture of her mom, with a "She's doing better!" And other days I would get no response at all. I knew she was facing her greatest heartbreak, and I also knew I wasn't the friend she needed at that time. I simply couldn't be, because I didn't know how to be. Instead of leaning in, I did what I knew how to do best, and retreated when it got hard.

Then one afternoon I got a text from our mutual friend. Hospice had been called in. It was just before Mother's Day, and Crystal's mother's health had begun to decline quickly. I reached out, in the timid way I had always done, but this time I received a response I didn't expect.

You see, when I am uncertain of the future, I shut down.

When I'm overwhelmed, I get irritable and snippy.

When I am hurting, I just want to be left alone.

But not Crystal—she let me in. In fact, she didn't just text me back an update; she extended an invite. And not just any invite—an invitation to sit with her dying mother at her bedside.

In that moment I knew I had to do something different if I wanted things to be different. I wanted a friendship in which I could be vulnerable and honest, and to deeply love her, and be loved by her. I didn't want to hide myself anymore, and I didn't want to live as a fearful or untrusting person. So I had to go for it. I had to go all in.

That afternoon forever changed the way I view friendships. I got to spend a few hours with my friend and her family in a way that I will never forget.

I rubbed her mother's feet.

I prayed with them.

I did their dishes.

I cried with her.

I even laughed with her.

And, the most precious thing of all, I heard them talk about their trust in the Lord.

As I went home that night, I grieved for my friend and her family, but I was even more overwhelmed by God's love. I didn't deserve that afternoon. I hadn't been that friend Crystal had needed. But the reality was, *it wasn't ever about me.*

Crystal's mother loved her country and she loved her family, but, above all, she loved the Lord. And looking back, I see that my friend was able to extend this love and grace to me because her mother was a Proverbs 31 woman. That kind of love—well, it all starts and ends with Jesus.

In Galatians, Paul wrote a letter to the church reminding them that, as believers, they were a part of a family that was equipped by the Spirit to fulfill the law, which is to love God and then others. To do this, Scripture says in Galatians 6:2 that we are to carry each other's burdens.

That's what my friend and her family did. They let me in to help carry their burden. And by doing so, we all felt more of God's love upon us. You see, we all carry burdens. Maybe not physical but perhaps emotional or financial. Sometimes we go through seasons when these burdens become too much to carry on our own. And while God's Spirit gives us the power and strength to endure, God also created relationships so we could carry these burdens together.

I think, for many of us, we fear asking for help because the world tries to pressure us into thinking that we are weak, ill-equipped, or too needy if we reach out and invite someone into our struggles. So we dry our eyes and power through because we don't want to inconvenience anyone. We withdraw and isolate to live with the lie that we aren't carrying a burden but rather we *are* the burden. But, friend, you are not a nuisance.

Later that week Crystal's mother would be reunited with God, but her legacy lives on. When I asked my friend for permission to share this story, she revealed to me that she realized she just needed to surrender. She had to get uncomfortable and *allow* people to love on her. Crystal says now how grateful she is that she invited others in, because if she hadn't, she would have missed out on all the blessings God provided then and continues to provide now.

God wants to bless you even in your pain, but it is your choice whether you will open your arms (or home) to receive it. When we choose to isolate, we settle into a vulnerable position for the Enemy to come in and attack us while we are down.

If you are naturally the caretaker in your relationships, it will be challenging to invite a friend in instead of managing any pain or hurt on your own. It takes practicing vulnerability and, of course, discerning who you will allow in and when. But it almost always involves taking a risk.

If you're anything like me, and you are used to bailing when things get a little too hard, or maybe you have messed up some good friendships because you didn't know how to steward them well, I want to encourage you: It isn't too late. Restoration is possible. Fighting for the good friendships is important.

We don't have to have it all figured out. We are going to fail each other. We won't know all the answers, and it won't always make sense. You are going to trust the wrong friend, and she will hurt you. You are going to mess up and hurt her too. But if we can lean on the Lord, he will help us through. He can be trusted, always.

The truth is that I am still hesitant to be in relationship with other women. My initial response is almost always to pull away, especially in seasons when we are asked to carry each other's burdens. I have a hard time letting anyone in too close, but I am getting better about this. When I notice I want to shut down, I remember I don't have to, because boundaries help me to show up in relationships as my best self. This means no longer withdrawing when it gets weird or hard. It means no longer isolating just because that feels easier. It means fighting to be a good friend before expecting to have one. It means choosing to work it out whenever possible, even with the crummy relationships, because sometimes those crummy ones are good ones in disguise. More than anything, it means allowing God to uncomplicate my friendships; because what he has for me is always way better than what I could ever secure on my own.

BURDENS VERSUS LOADS

You may be wondering, *Wait, I thought we weren't meant to carry each other's stuff. Isn't that how boundaries get blurred and codependency creeps back in?* Great question. Thankfully, we have Scripture to bring us clarity.

If we look deeper into Galatians, God reveals to us further distinction and instruction: "For each one should carry their own load" (6:5).

Perhaps this illustration will help you. Consider the *burdens* as large boulders. My friend Crystal was carrying a large burden as her mother was losing her battle with cancer. We are meant to carry each other's burdens, as they are too heavy to carry on our own, and healthy boundaries allow us to carry each other's burdens safely and effectively. This may look like dropping off a meal, helping your friend with her kids, or starting a GoFundMe page to raise money for medical expenses. But we can carry each other's burdens when they arise only if we are primarily carrying our own *loads* each day.

> **We are meant to carry each other's burdens, as they are too heavy to carry on our own.**

Loads are your daily responsibilities; these are more like little backpacks—bills, schoolwork, jobs. Things get complicated when you or I try to take on other people's loads (backpacks) as though they are major burdens (boulders) to shoulder together. *They aren't.*

Healthy boundaries ensure that I am consistently carrying my own backpack, and you are carrying yours. This doesn't mean you don't help others with their smaller loads on occasion. It means you commit to keep ownership over your own responsibilities, and you encourage others to do the same. If I try to carry my daily load *and* yours, problems arise. Why? Because I can carry only so much, and it is likely that if I attempt to carry something of yours, I am forced to set something of my own down. Over time you may come to expect my help, and I may expect you to need my help, and we both grow less capable at managing our own loads. Here, we open our relationship to bitterness, confusion, and codependency.[1]

This is why boundaries are so beneficial. They keep your backpack or load on your shoulders, with all your daily load stuff, and mine on my own. This separateness ensures that when a bigger boulder comes either your way or mine, we have the capacity and confidence to shoulder it together. This was part of God's design.

FELLOWSHIP

When my mother wrote the letter to me for my birthday about her childhood, she mentioned how my grandmother was not very interested in celebrating. What I think she meant, and what I can reflect now about my own mother and even myself, is that we resisted hospitality. In part, I believe this was due to shame about some of the activities occurring in and outside of our home. Regardless, I didn't get much modeling in this area, so when I became a married adult woman with children, hospitality felt foreign.

I have learned a lot in the last few years on this topic. First, that fellowship doesn't happen by accident. I had to pursue fellowship with other women, specifically with other families. It's very easy to close my doors and do my own life independently. And for many years my family did. We went to church on Sundays and smiled and greeted others in the lobby, only to return home to tackle our to-do lists. Next-door neighbors would pass by on the street as my kids played in the front yard, but it never went further than a simple, "Sure is a beautiful day, isn't it?" I would see other moms at school during drop-off, or I would run into an old high school classmate in the supermarket checkout line, but nothing ever went below surface level. I valued all these relationships, but I didn't know how to develop them outside of what they already were. There it was again, that awkward dating feeling.

Since I knew growing these relationships would take intentionality, I started a tradition of hosting Sunday spaghetti dinners. Hospitality became the bridge toward boosting our levels of fellowship. And everyone likes spaghetti, so I began inviting folks over.

A simple text would go out: "Sunday spaghetti! Come on by! Casual!"

At first I worried that they wouldn't come. And then I worried that if they came, what would we talk about? Or, worse, how long would they stay? For a while it felt just as odd as I had imagined. But over time it didn't. No longer were they just people we passed by in life. They became friends. My kids became friends with their kids. Slowly, we started doing life together.

No, we didn't have everything in common. But we had the important things in common. We followed Christ, and our shared convictions, values, and behaviors reflected that. It began to feel as though we were on the same team, not only to worship God on Sunday but to live out his will and go out and do his work in the world.

I have learned that hospitality is not the same thing as entertaining. Both have value and their rightful place, but they are vastly different.

Entertaining says, "Look at my fancy tablescape," and hospitality says, "Can you bring a dish? It's potluck."

Entertaining says, "I've cooked all day," and hospitality says, "I just put the spaghetti on—can you grab the paper plates from the pantry?"

Entertaining says, "I want you to be my guest," and hospitality says, "I want you to become my friend."

I think, for many of us, we don't host others in our homes because we fear what they may find out about us. We worry that who they see on Sunday at church, in the grocery store, or at our children's school suddenly won't match up with who they discover when they step over the threshold of our front door. But this fear is also why we may miss out on what they *do* find out about us: We are loving. Compassionate. Thoughtful. Warm. And *very human*. We are just like them—flawed and in desperate need of Jesus.

And you know what else? We get to find out about who they are outside of a quick hello or casual encounter. When we lay down our fears, pride, and insecurities, we get to hear about their sister who is getting married next spring, or how they felt when their kid started their first day of college. We get to watch football together and laugh at how silly the dog acts when the kids tease him. We get to mentor them and they get to mentor us. We get to pray together and eat together and be together; but none of this is possible unless we first become willing to open our doors as an extension of opening our hearts. It is never not a good thing to get to do this life together, because according to God, it's always done better together anyway.

Let us not, as Hebrews says, "[give] up meeting together" (10:25).

Don't talk yourself out of what God has for you through hospitality. It isn't about opening your home just to serve others. It's about caring for each other and building community through intentional fellowship. As Will Guidara writes, "Service is black and white; hospitality is color."[2] Step out in faith and create some color in your relationships! Take a risk, throw some pasta in a pot of boiling water, and send out a few invites. Learn to trust that others don't love you because your house is clean, or your kids are just so, or you entertain with a five-star meal made from scratch. Often, others love you because none of this is true, and because, well . . . *you let them.*

ACKNOWLEDGE & CONFRONT

1. What surprised you most about the differences between a burden and a load? Explain.
2. Do you allow others to shoulder your large burdens? How do you typically respond when you go through a challenging season? Do you isolate or pretend you're okay?
3. Have you ever stepped in to carry someone's load or "small backpack" when this was a responsibility that they needed to carry? How did that turn out?
4. Were your caregivers hospitable? Why or why not?
5. What holds you back from being more hospitable now?

14

Triggers

I ARRIVED AT MELISSA'S HOUSE FOR A SMALL get-together. She was far more than just a friend; she was the wife of our lead pastor and had been mentoring me for the past year. This gathering had a purpose: to discuss the upcoming year of women's events that she would lead at church. The handful of women in the group were not just volunteers; they were other leaders who I was growing to admire. As we nibbled on charcuterie, the topic of disciplining our children came up. Slowly, each woman began to share briefly what had worked for her through the different seasons of motherhood; I sat on the edge of my seat attentively soaking it all in.

I didn't want to admit it at the time, but my husband and I had lost all authority in our home. We were on the defensive, feeling outnumbered, as our girls were now four and six and the twins were barely two. It wasn't a quick loss; it happened slowly—casual back talk, an unfinished chore, a lack of gratitude, a shove of a sibling. We began to walk on eggshells around each other, and this lack of authority was causing not only disruption in how we parented but also strain on our marriage. Because of our uncertainty about what to do, we defaulted to patterns that we knew best—like yelling.

"Clean this up now, because I said so!"

"Keep your hands off your sister!"

"Would be nice if you'd say thank you!"

"Go to your room!"

That evening I shared my lack of confidence with the other women at the table. It was a safe, nonjudgmental space, which helped me open up. Melissa then said, "Often when we get angry, it isn't because we are *using* our authority—it is because we fear we are losing it."

Ouch. That's what this was.

Fear again.

We were trying to discipline their sinful nature with sinful parenting.

We were correcting their snarky comments with snarky ones of our own.

We were addressing a shove of a sibling with an impatient grab of their arm.

We were confronting their anger with our own anger.

Our house was not the loving, safe, peaceful, and playful home I had envisioned. But I didn't know how to get from where we were *to that*—from the anxious, irritated, annoyed, and weary parent to the one who felt equipped and capable.

I began reading *Habits of the Household* by Justin Whitmel Earley, and God truly spoke to me through it. I felt an ache arise, one signaling that I had gotten far off track. I had grown an overdeveloped sense of my child being "good," and this mindset, reinforced by some secular parenting styles, was causing devastation inside our home.

My children had begun to lead, not my husband and I.

I wanted so badly to create an environment where my children felt safe and seen. I wanted them to be heard. I wanted them to feel free to be kids. And while all of this does matter, I allowed it to go a bit too far. I realized that kids feel most safe, seen, heard, and free within the constraints of limitations. After some self-reflection, prayer, and many conversations with my husband, I had to admit that fear is what had placed our children at the center of our family.

I wanted to understand what was at the root of this fear. It was then that I finally got honest with myself: *I was trying to manage my own childhood deprivation by overcompensating for theirs.* Our day-to-day activities revolved around them—their moods, their wants, their needs. I began to place them on a pedestal in hopes it would provide for them all of what I didn't get, yet this just cultivated a family culture of misplaced authority. It became clear to me that I also wasn't just trying to manage the ongoing activities and interactions within our home; I was working to manage my children's feelings—a pattern of behavior I was oh-so familiar with from before. You see, when a child isn't used to hearing no, he will often grow into an adult who can't tell himself or others no. This was me. Our relationships were founded on boundaryless behavior, and we were all feeling the consequences of it.

What did this look like?

It looked like allowing my child to scream because they were angry.

It looked like allowing my child to keep her room messy because she was tired.

It looked like allowing my child to shift the entire mood of the house because he was unhappy.

It looked like allowing myself to cancel date night because my child didn't want me to go out.

It looked like catering to their impatient demands promptly just to keep the peace.

It looked like allowing my child to hit her sibling without a consequence.

It looked like allowing my child to not say please, thank you, or sorry because he didn't understand what being polite, grateful, or remorseful meant yet.

My children aren't inherently good, and I can't *make* them good by being a perfect parent. I think, somewhere deep inside, I believed that if I ignored the behavior in our home, it would suddenly get better or just go away. I was back to pretending things were okay when they weren't, just as I had as a child. I had to face the truth: my children were sinful upon conception (Ps. 51:5). Left to their own devices, they will self-destruct, and just like you and me, they need healthy boundaries. God has lent us these children to love, nurture, and protect, which requires intentionality and work. Until they learn to depend on God for safe parameters, they will depend on us for them.

So my husband and I began to reorder our home, which started by first identifying what we as parents wanted our family culture to look and feel like. We even sat down with our older girls one afternoon while enjoying smoothies together and wrote out a list of words that we wanted our family to pursue and one day represent (on a napkin, of course).

> **Until they learn to depend on God for safe parameters, they will depend on us for them.**

Knowing our values as a family mattered because it not only clarified what we wanted to guard and protect, but it gave us a vision for the direction we were headed. Here the day-to-day choices and behaviors didn't seem so insignificant anymore. In fact, it's the day-to-day choices and behaviors that determine what we would one day represent and, more importantly, *who* we would represent as a family unit.

Kind
thankful
peaceful
respectfu
joyful
playful
patient

What did this look like? It looked like going on our date together, no matter how hard the kids kicked and screamed about it, because we valued the health of our marriage and knew it would bless our children. It meant enforcing household chores to be done, regardless of our children's moods, because caring for our belongings is a practice of wise stewardship. It meant encouraging them to seek forgiveness after a squabble with each other, even if they didn't want to, because we can model the overarching narrative of redemption, forgiveness, and reconciliation played out in the Bible. It meant training them to think, speak, and act in ways that honor God, which continues to be both our greatest challenge and yet our greatest privilege.

At first my children's resistance was high, because change can feel threatening. But they have adjusted and so have we. Over time, taking back our authority in the home as parents allowed us all to actually enjoy spending time together as opposed to dreading it. Instead of being irritated or anxious, we had more bandwidth to engage in small rituals of connection, such as affection and play. The homelife I had hoped to create for my children—one full of love, safety, peace, and playfulness—was no longer just a dream but a reality.

MICROMANAGING

While our home was starting to feel more peaceful and my outside relationships were growing safer, I still struggled with moments of anger that I didn't know what to do with.

I noticed the anger whenever a kid would throw a tantrum and my fists would clench, or in the irritation that would bubble up in my chest when my husband got home late from work. At times contempt would even creep in if a friend interrupted our plan to do something spontaneous.

One year as my husband's birthday was coming up, I decided to throw him a small get-together at a nearby restaurant, inviting friends to join us on the deck overlooking the water. A friend asked if she could help, and while I had most of the details nailed down, I told her it would be fine for her to pick up some balloons on her way. That evening she arrived holding rainbow-colored balloons, and while I laughed on the outside, I was red-hot on the inside. *Didn't I tell her the theme was black and white?* I tucked the balloons in a far, far back corner, exclaiming, "Oh, thank you! Wow, I can't believe how much the wind has picked up. Let's put them over here for safekeeping!"

This was one of many instances when my anger was distracting me from enjoying the good happening around me. I couldn't be present or delight in the company of those I loved most because I was always far too concerned about the way things were being done or how they were perceived.

My kids weren't being unreasonable when they threw a fit about the pink cup instead of the green one; they were simply being toddlers. My husband wasn't being disrespectful when he got home late for dinner; he was just delayed by the train. And my sweet friend wasn't being inconsiderate when she brought those colorful balloons; she was just having fun. That is when I realized my anger was a symptom of a much deeper issue—*my need for control.*

These triggers were moments of tension that started to erode me from the inside out. And for a while, instead of admitting my need for control, I chose to blame those closest to me for my anger.

"If you'd just put her down for a nap when I said so, she wouldn't be so cranky."

"If you just left work a few minutes early, you wouldn't be late getting home."

"If she'd just paid more attention, she would have stuck to the party theme."

This becomes exhausting because living on the defense is a full-time job. My pride was on full blast, barking orders and criticisms. I often felt deflated and disappointed, weighed down by the shame of my own behavior. The less joy I felt, the more I worked to micromanage every detail of my life and the lives of those around me. I wanted to be happy, but more than that I wanted to be perfect.

Perfectionism

It was one of those mornings when, after thirteen hours of solid sleep, the children *still* wake up cranky. The sort of day where no matter what you cook, it's "disgusting"; no matter when you change their diapers, they scream bloody murder while doing an alligator roll. It was one of those days when everything from morning to night is hard, and I was emotionally, physically, and spiritually spent. It was the ideal setting for my control and anger to be on full display.

It showed up in the moment when I hollered at my oldest daughter to "Get in the car, nooooow, we are late!"

It showed up when I rolled my eyes at my husband in disrespect.

It showed up when I snatched the dirty clothes off the ground, only to toss them into the hamper and slam the laundry room door shut in disgust.

It showed up when I replied to a girlfriend in an impatient and rude way.

My anger was a form of protection. If I could be angry, I didn't have to ask for help. If I could be angry, I wouldn't have to let others in. If I could be angry, I could stay mad because I was the one having to do it all. If I could be angry, I could continue to blame others for my unhappiness.

Somewhere deep inside I still harbored the belief that if I tried hard enough, I could be perfect. Each morning I would wake and try my hardest, only to go to bed each night with shame that I failed. I never once considered that I couldn't do it because I wasn't designed to do it. I had a habit of forgetting that I am human, deeply flawed, and in need of a saving grace. A grace that sometimes I don't think I need, which simply confirms that I do.

I pressured everyone in my life with the same pressure I put on myself. And when they didn't meet my expectations of perfection, just as I couldn't meet my own, anger would ensue.

On the especially hard days, I still get slapped in the face by humility. I have learned that humility is the tool to use to kill off pride for good. The extent to which I began to accept my own imperfections and surrender myself to be washed over by God's grace is the same extent to which I can accept the imperfections of those around me. This is how the joy seeps in. I didn't need to be in control to feel safe anymore. I could learn to live each day, no matter how challenging, knowing he is sovereign.

Perhaps we don't need ourselves and each other to be perfect. Maybe all we need is to know a perfect God. A God in whom we can seek and find solace and refuge. To rest in a relationship that cannot and will not fail us. To trust that we don't have to people-please, perform, or pretend in order to be loved. The goal is to be a good and faithful servant (Matt. 25:23), not a perfect one.

Reparenting

One of the most helpful tools I have discovered when facing my own imperfections or daily triggers has been learning how to reparent myself. Maybe you aren't a parent yet, or don't plan to be, but you feel angry, disappointed, or hurt a lot in your relationships. If so, reparenting can be helpful.

Reparenting isn't meant to point the finger at your parents;

instead, it is an opportunity for you to take responsibility for your current unhappiness. Maybe you have yet to accept that you are good and loved, you are adored and valued, you are enough and worthy.

Reparenting may mean different things to different people, but I have found it to be especially freeing. It not only sets the others you love free; it sets *you* free. By choosing to reparent yourself, you finally give to yourself what you have always wanted and needed but perhaps never got.

When I am triggered by someone or something, I can look to what I can control and let go of what I can't. Trying to control all that was happening around me was a skill I brought with me from childhood and a means to secure some sort of safety in predictability. Triggers, I have learned, are often not about the person or situation in front of me at all. Instead, this emotional flooding points me back to the unmet needs in my past.

BREATHE. PRAY. ACT.

Triggers tend to be accompanied by some sort of emotional reaction inside the body and are often more distressing when they come as a surprise. If I consider the party and the colorful balloons, I can clearly see now how the spontaneity caused me to feel out of control, and that lack of control left me feeling unsafe. But it wasn't about the balloons or my friend. As I exercise emotional maturity, I can see a trigger like this for what it is and not be held hostage by it any longer. How? By remembering that my safety isn't found in others, their behavior, or their perceptions of me. Here, I am better positioned to let the joy in and to delight alongside my friend and her playful balloon choice.

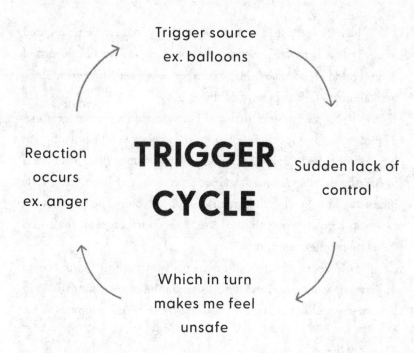

Trigger source
ex. balloons

TRIGGER CYCLE

Reaction occurs ex. anger

Sudden lack of control

Which in turn makes me feel unsafe

For you, something like this may not throw you into an angry spiral. Perhaps when you feel out of control, you freeze up or want to shut down and hide. This is what some psychologists refer to as your "stress signature," and becoming aware of your own stress signature will be helpful in managing it. When I am triggered, I notice the anger rising up inside me and I walk myself through a simple yet effective process.

First, I breathe.

There are many options for conscious breathing, but my favorite method is called *box breathing*. It includes visualizing a box and then breathing and counting as you work your way around the edges of the box in your mind. This technique has many benefits, the greatest being that it helps you return your body back to recovery after the automatic stress response.[1]

When you feel safe in both mind and body, you can better respond in a way that is more Christlike. As noted earlier, the Greek root of "sound mind" is from *sózó*, "to be saved or delivered," and *phrén*, "one's mental inclination or pattern of thought."

As I was researching further, I came to find a deeper meaning. The root *phrén* is also the root word in *diaphragm*.[2] The diaphragm is a dome-shaped muscle at the base of your lungs that, when used to breathe, is known to reduce blood pressure and heart rate, while increasing how much rich oxygen is in your blood. This inner organ can help regulate your physical life, your heartbeat, and the blood traveling through your body.

Breathing consciously can be the pathway back to a sound mind in a triggering moment, and with a sound mind you are more likely to behave in ways that are God-honoring in your relationships.

Then I pray.

This step isn't elaborate, which is why it is often overlooked. Sometimes it's just muttering the words "Jesus, help me" under my breath. If I am able, I try to pray for guidance and wisdom. This may sound like "God, I am feeling triggered right now, and my anger is taking over. Please help me respond how you would." At the very least, I put on an Anne Wilson song and sing out those lyrics with the windows down. I remind myself that I no longer have to fear my feelings, because I don't have to fear what I already have authority over. Anger itself isn't a bad thing; it's what I choose to do with the anger that has the potential to be bad. I can feel angry, then access what I need and communicate that instead of my anger. Maybe I need to communicate to myself that I am not a scared little girl anymore and that I am safe now. Maybe I need help. Maybe I need a hug. Maybe I need to sit down for a meal. Maybe I need to commit to less.

Finally, I take action.

I start by exercising self-control. This may mean different things at different times, but it always means taking authority over my anger. It may look like sitting my child down for discipline using a tone and body posture that isn't threatening or scary for them. It may mean refraining from discussing something with my husband in a heated moment and letting my emotions settle so I don't say something that I will regret later. It may mean pressing pause before responding in irritation when a coworker sends a text asking me to cover her shift (again).

Then I tend to my own inner child. After years of doing this work, I can see the benefit of caring for my inner child through reparenting her in small, consistent ways. All this means is giving myself the love, acceptance, and safety I needed as a child now as an adult. This may look like running myself a hot bath after a long, draining day of parenting. It may be writing out my thoughts in a journal or going for a walk. It may be as simple as getting to bed early, or making it to that doctor's appointment, because my health matters too. It doesn't have to be elaborate or expensive, but it should be consistent.

Lately, the most powerful way I tend to my inner child is through personal words of affirmation. When I remind myself that I am enough, it's as if the anger no longer has a hold on me. Sometimes, in a hard moment, I don't believe the words I am saying to myself. But then I remember my own kid doesn't always feel grateful when I remind her to say thank you either. Sometimes we have to just trust that if we let the words flow, the feelings will soon follow. In those trying moments, when I don't feel entirely loved or valued, or like I am doing a good job, I look to rely on God's feelings about me over my own.

Joyce Meyer shares verses to turn to in these moments:

I am chosen by God who called me out of the darkness of sin and into the light and life of Christ so I can proclaim the excellence and greatness of who He is (1 Peter 2:9).

I am born again—spiritually transformed, renewed and set apart for God's purpose—through the living and everlasting word of God (1 Peter 1:23).

I am God's workmanship, created in Christ to do good works that He has prepared for me to do (Ephesians 2:10).

I am renewed in the knowledge of God and no longer want to live in my old ways or nature before I accepted Christ (Colossians 3:9–10).

I am a joint-heir with Christ, and I am more than a conqueror through Him who loves me (Romans 8:17, 37).

I am saved by God's grace, raised up with Christ and seated with Him in heavenly places (Ephesians 2:5–6; Colossians 2:12).

I am greatly loved by God (John 3:16; Ephesians 2:4; Colossians 3:12; 1 Thessalonians 1:4).

I am strengthened with all power according to His glorious might (Colossians 1:11).[3]

And you are all of this in him too.

Speaking these words over myself helps to shift my heart posture, and this becomes a blessing for both me and my relationships. It reflects trusting God in his decision to pick me for this moment, right here, right now. God can't make mistakes, after all. So why should I live as one?

All of this can appear quite simple, which is why it can also be difficult. You may be wondering if there is ever a time that recurring triggers reflect an unhealthy situation or relationship. The short answer is yes. It is important to consistently commune with God over this. You can and should take time to consider if God is asking you to lean in and work through triggers within a relationship as a means to grow you, or if continual triggers are a sign that a relationship is unstable or unsafe. Ask him, and he will guide your steps.

If we commit to doing some of this work within to heal, we will no longer look for others to do it for us. This is how we withstand the temptation to blame our family or closest relationships for our unhealthy behavior or unhappiness. It is also how we eventually take authority over our triggers, using them as a means to better understand how we can love ourselves and others in the ways he has called us to. You may even find that some triggers bring you to the end of yourself, and I am beginning to wonder if that's the point. It is at the end of ourselves that we are brought back to him.

ACKNOWLEDGE & CONFRONT

1. Did you have limits as a child? Are you able to tell yourself and others no now as an adult? Explain.
2. Review the trigger cycle. When is the last time you were triggered? How did you feel out of control? And how did this lack of control or safety make you behave?
3. Take a moment to look up the box breathing method on YouTube and work through a round now.
4. What can you do today to tend to your inner child? Write down some ideas (run a bath, speak words of affirmation, rest, journal, make an overdue doctor's appointment, etc.).
5. Choose a verse from the list provided in this chapter and hang it where you will see it often. Which did you choose and why?

15

If Possible

I LIVE IN A SMALL SEASIDE TOWN WITH COASTAL beaches that attract tourists from all over the world. We locals joke that *we live where you vacation*, and it's true. Our beaches aren't just popular for their pristine white sand and aqua-blue waters, but they are also known for being one of the top turtle-nesting beaches in the world. In fact, our South Florida beaches have housed up to thirteen thousand loggerhead sea turtle nests in one nesting season alone.[1]

Female loggerheads spend up to twenty years maturing and growing in open waters, migrating closer to nearby beaches only to forage. Then, when it is time, they will begin a journey upwards of eight thousand miles to return to the *same beach* where they themselves hatched, to mate and eventually lay their own eggs.

While the male loggerheads never return to sand, the females do rarely—only at night to prepare their nests and lay eggs.[2] If you are as fortunate as I have been, you can witness this incredible process firsthand. During nesting season, if you take a walk along the shore after sunset, you are likely to come across some loggerhead tracks. And nearby you may still find a female loggerhead digging out a hole with her hind legs, flinging sand all over. She will lay three to five nests, all about two weeks apart, with each nest containing about one hundred eggs.[3] And while that sounds like a lot of hatchlings, not all of them will survive. Many factors, such as climate, biology, and nearby predators, have an impact on whether the hatchling makes it safely to sea.[4] But she won't ever know who makes it and who doesn't, because she is long gone before they hatch, having slipped back into the open waters.

So what do the turtle hatchlings do without anyone there to help guide them?

Well, after about two months in their nest, they hatch out of their eggs and dig their way to the sandy surface, making a beeline dash to the water's edge. This is what marine biologists refer to as the turtle's first "trek," which imprints their home beach to memory. During this trek they are under threat of not only dehydration but being eaten by crabs, birds, and other animals that prey on hatchlings.[5]

Perhaps you, too, can relate to being abandoned and left to figure it out on your own. Maybe you wished that you had someone there to gently guide you, protect you, and nurture you, fending off the hard and scary sides of this world. On the other hand, maybe you never felt like you had a nest *at all*. Or the one you did have never felt very safe. Yet for some unexplainable reason, no matter how far you venture out in life, you feel drawn back to it. As with these hatchlings, that original imprint is strong. If so, I get it. I see you.

I know what it feels like to love through obligation and to return to people or places that can no longer hold me. I have struggled through seasons of guilt for chasing after my own dreams, goals, or pursuits. If I am not careful, I can begin to focus on all that did or didn't happen in the past, missing out on today. Please know, friend, it isn't too late for you to start your own journey. You can venture out into unknown waters, only to return home if it is safe for you.

And if you are a mother, you can begin to do the work now to create a home that your children want to return to, as it's never too late to begin. You can be the consistent, predictable, soft, and safe place for them to land. You can remind your maturing child that her job is to explore and mature toward independence; after all, children were created to serve God, *not you*. Of course, their eventual leaving will inadvertently cause you pain. But that discomfort isn't theirs to bear—it's yours. You can tend to the discomfort in ways that are responsible, like seeking a safe friend, attending therapy, or starting a new hobby.

For those of you who don't have children and never plan to, or those of you who are single and unsure of what is next, there is still so much God has in store for you. He wants to be your safe place, and he wants to help develop safety in and through you. Part of stepping into the blessings of your next chapter will be done through grieving what you didn't get so that you can start welcoming and preparing for what is yet to come.

GRIEVING

Have you ever heard of the Japanese art of *kintsugi*? It is a four-hundred-year-old art technique of putting broken pottery pieces back together with gold.[6] What once would be considered a wasted piece of pottery now becomes not only more beautiful but more valuable. The lacquer and gold don't just repair the piece to make it look as if it were never broken but instead highlight the "scars" as part of its new design. The brokenness is what increases its worth.

> Your grief doesn't indicate that you don't trust God. It indicates that you aren't God.

Part of your very own breaking is allowing yourself to grieve. Your grief doesn't indicate that you don't trust God. It indicates that you aren't God. And part of your healing, like the art of kintsugi, will be allowing God to put you back together.

You and I are the work of God's hands—the hands of the finest potter (Lam. 4:2). There will be seasons and situations when you must be tried by the fire. We will all stumble, fall, and at times break. But this life, the challenging relationships, the mess-ups and mistakes, your broken pieces, well, they will *never define your value*. What God has in store for you, to put you back together, preciously, precisely, piece by piece, is a gift. Your worth is defined by him and his workmanship in you, not by your broken parts or past. To think, he could use any material he wanted, but he chooses only the finest gold of love and grace. It is the means by which he will restore you and me to honor and dignity, again and again. We are, after all, his most valued masterpieces (Eph. 2:10 NLT).

If you are breaking today, and in that brokenness you are uncertain about what is next for you and some of your hardest relationships, I want to encourage you. You don't have to allow your broken pieces to dictate your next move. You can proclaim the beauty that God is doing in and around you, even if you don't see the finished piece of art yet, knowing that when he is done with you, you will be more valuable than before.

GRACE

There is a big difference between accepting people and waiting for them to change.

Waiting for others to change looks like lots of passive absorption. You hope that if you wait it out long enough, maybe they will acknowledge their ways and begin to behave differently.

Acceptance means you accept them right now, as they are, and not based on who you expect or hope them to be one day. Based on this full acceptance, you then determine what you will and will not tolerate in their presence. You also allow yourself to grow and change, whether they decide to come with you or not.

Often, what is in the way of your relationships becoming the best they can be is *you*. You become your very worst enemy. You assume the role of caretaker, fixer, micromanager. But doing this means you will never be who you were created to be, and your relationships will never be what they were created to be. The only thing that can save you from yourself is God.

God's grace is powerful, restorative, relational, and very much at times *uncomfortable*. This can be hard to remember because it doesn't always fit the model of what the world says about love. God cares more about getting you to eternity with him than whether or not you like how he gets you there. This is the kind of love and grace we must strive for.

We need a paradigm shift in how we perceive relationships. Once we fully comprehend a relationship's innate purpose, we can then begin to appreciate relationships for what they really are. As Paul David Tripp writes, "We need to be trained not to see relationships as belonging to us for our happiness, but rather as workrooms in which the Lord can do his transforming work."[7]

Part of allowing our relationships to shape us in the way God designed them—to become workrooms to transform us—is by first grieving the relationships we thought we had—or that we never got to experience—and extending godlike grace in the ones we do. It's a daily commitment, that's for sure. But it is one that will be necessary to pass on the legacy you hope to leave those around you and after you.

LEGACY

God wants your cooperation in writing your next chapter, and the one after that, and after that. Maybe you are surrounded by people you love who are unsupportive of your healing process. That's okay. It doesn't mean you can't do it. You are still allowed to write a legacy that you and God are proud of. One that honors all that he is.

Wherever you are, you are touching the lives of those around you. And through those relationships, God wants to use you. He hasn't forgotten about you. You are worthy and valuable to him. Every breath of yours is an opportunity.

Legacy writing is simply becoming intentional about ensuring that what was done to you won't become you. It is you taking authority over your heartbreak or loss and using it for something greater than yourself.

Your legacy is a culmination of your core values and actions. It is directly affected by the healthy new patterns you are establishing and stewarding right now. If you don't like what you inherited, you get to change that. You get to choose what you will pass on and what will end with you. Let me ask you, *What will people miss most about you when you are gone?*

RECONCILIATION

On the outside, I was doing all the work. I was setting the boundaries. I was exercising self-control in my relationships. I was reminding myself often what was my responsibility and what wasn't. I was checking all the boxes, but I still didn't *feel free.*

What gives?

You may be familiar with the story of Joseph. In short, Joseph was treated a bit more special by his parents, and this brought his brothers much jealousy. We learn that Joseph's brothers sought to kill him by throwing him into a pit to die, but they eventually sold him into Egyptian slavery instead. After some time in prison, Joseph made himself known and useful to the pharaoh of Egypt by interpreting his dreams, and later he was elected as Pharaoh's highest official.

Before long, a famine broke out, which provoked Joseph's brothers to leave Canaan and seek out food in Egypt. The ten men bowed before Joseph, but Joseph did not reveal his identity until he was certain that they had changed, and not until he could confirm that his youngest brother, Benjamin, who had been left back home, was safe. Then Joseph, certain of his brothers' true repentance, revealed himself.

"I am your brother Joseph, the one you sold into Egypt!" (Gen. 45:4).

All of the brothers suddenly broke down in tears, embracing one another.

And Joseph did what I don't think I could do.

He comforted them by saying,

And now, do not be distressed and do not be angry with yourselves for selling me here, because it was to save lives that God sent me ahead of you. For two years now there has been famine in the land, and for the next five years there will be no plowing and reaping. But God sent me ahead of you to preserve for you a remnant on earth and to save your lives by a great deliverance. (Gen. 45:5–7)

Joseph had every right to be hurt. To hold a resentment. To throw his brothers into prison or have them killed. But instead, he understood the larger picture. He trusted that God had sent him there. And while he didn't excuse his brothers' wrongdoing, he did choose to believe that God was still in charge and that his ways were good.

Joseph then went on to say, "You intended to harm me, but God intended it for good to accomplish what is now being done, the saving of many lives" (Gen. 50:20).

―――――――

We can all relate to some degree to feeling betrayed, lied to, and abandoned, just as Joseph was. I am sure there were many nights when he was lonely, afraid, and confused. I can imagine him replaying the scenarios in his head about his brothers—what was said, and even what wasn't said. Maybe his thoughts spiraled about all the different ways things could have been done or should have been done. I imagine he was also tempted to allow his heart to harden; after all, he'd suffered the cruelest injustices. And maybe for a while his heart did grow weary and cold.

I wondered to myself whether Joseph had ever been tempted to feel guilty about all that God was blessing him with. But if we look back, Scripture reveals Joseph's obedience to live free of unforgiveness and bitterness *long before he ever faced his brothers*. In fact, the names of Joseph's two sons reflected the healing God had already started in his heart.

> Joseph named his firstborn Manasseh and said, "It is because God has made me forget all my trouble and all my father's household." The second son he named Ephraim and said, "It is because God has made me fruitful in the land of my suffering." (Gen. 41:51–52)

Forgetful.

Fruitful.

There it was. This was it.

Joseph was free because he chose to be free.

What God revealed to me in this story of Joseph is that I was living only partially obedient to God. Joseph didn't find healing because of his reconciliation with his brothers. This healing had come long beforehand, through God alone. And Joseph was not only healed; he had become fruitful. He was living assured of God's plan even with little assurance that there would ever come a day that he would face his brothers and witness their changed hearts.

I don't know about you, but there are some things I am still working to forget as well as some fruit I can't wait to one day bear.

I believe many of us wait for reconciliation, admittance of wrongdoing, or an apology before we allow ourselves to experience this kind of healing. We want to know if the person who has hurt us is aware of the pain they have caused. We wonder if they are changed and wait for this confirmation before we claim the freedom and healing that is ours right now in Christ.

Yet like Joseph, we don't have to wait. We can choose to fix our eyes on and remain obedient to God's promise found in Isaiah, that Jesus came to mend our broken hearts so we could now live free (61:1).

WISE DISCERNMENT

My children have disagreements, as do most, I imagine. And while I do my best to help them navigate those situations, what I have found most interesting is their desire to reconcile regardless of who was to blame. It's as if their longing to be together supersedes their hurt or anger toward each other.

This brings me back to one of the first concepts I highlighted in this book: *We are created to be in relationship with each other.* We are hardwired to reconnect, and sometimes this pull grows stronger when we experience some time apart.

There will be moments with certain people when space is necessary. Disconnection may serve your relationship, as it helps you realign who you are, clarifies your responsibilities, and brings long-lasting benefit to you both. There will be times, however, when the space created between you and another person becomes permanent. And when this happens, it will be natural to experience a longing for them even if you know the relationship was not good.

Discernment is really all about the emotional health condition of your heart. When you learn to discern, you will begin to appreciate these longings as a design of our Creator and pursue him for comfort, refuge, and rest. Remember, he created you with this void and therefore only he can fill it. A good friend once told me that when I feel lonely, it's a reminder of an overdue appointment with God.

IF POSSIBLE...

We are asked by God to live in peace with others, yet this isn't the same as functioning as the peacekeeper in your relationships. Living in peace with others means pursuing forgiveness no matter how difficult that is. Forgiveness may not always lead to reconciliation, but it makes peace possible even when reconciliation is not.

"If it is possible, as far as it depends on you, live at peace with everyone" (Rom. 12:18).

You may be wondering, *Why should I have to pursue forgiveness, if someone else wronged me?* I get it, and sometimes I don't like this answer either, but it is because we have been forgiven. Humanity's first recorded relationship was broken, and this brokenness caused estrangement. God sent his Son to reconcile with us, out of love and through grace. When we choose to accept Jesus as our Savior, we are reconciled with him once again.

Some of your relationships right now may be broken, and this is causing a rift. It is disrupting your peace, and your heart has grown callous. You can pursue forgiveness with them and toward them; however, this may not bring reconciliation. Scripture tells us we are to live at peace when it is possible. And this may mean living life apart. Regardless of how many tears you've shed, prayers you've prayed, and attempts you've made, being in relationship together again is simply not an option. So what do you do?

You move on.

Reconciliation should never be made possible through the sudden abandonment of your boundaries. Like our reconciliation with God, it takes acceptance and turning toward one another. It takes two who are committed. Two who are trying. It requires work from both sides. You can't control another person's level of effort, commitment, and motivation. But you can be mindful of pursuing relationships at a pace that is safe and healthy. God will never ask you to leave him to pursue someone else. If a relationship is becoming a dividing wedge between you and your Creator, this is a warning that shouldn't be ignored.

Sometimes folks won't be able or willing. They are far from God, far from moving on, far from working through it. You can still ask God for forgiveness for your mistakes and seek their forgiveness for your failures. You can work to forgive them, knowing this takes intentionality and time. You can allow the experience to grow and shape you. Then you can let go of the guilt, knowing you are already reconciled with God, while surrendering this relationship over to him.

If a relationship is becoming a dividing wedge between you and your Creator, this is a warning that shouldn't be ignored.

I believe God will help you through whatever conflict you are up against right now. I know it is the most painful thing to live unreconciled with others. I imagine it is the same pain our heavenly Father feels when his children are lost and distant. I pray that if reconciliation is not possible, he brings you comfort and peace in that place instead.

While I have found a path of healing and have integrated the tools I have shared here with you, I would be lying if I told you that it always felt easy and uncomplicated. This journey isn't linear. It's not going to be clear and concise. It won't always feel good. I wish it did, for all of us. At times I hated letting go of the patterns of behavior that allowed me to love others the way I knew how, even when it left me hurting.

There are still relationships that I long to have restored. I still worry and wonder about loved ones who are far from God. I still occasionally feel guilty and at times even ache for climbing out of the crab bucket.

Perhaps the only thing more painful than an unreconciled relationship here is the thought of not having one with them in eternity. I will never not want to witness their freedom and healing in Christ. But I no longer live loyal to a fault. I believe God still heals, helps, and restores. Now I choose to trust in his timing and the ways in which he does what he does best.

If you are in a dark season of uncertainty, doubt, disappointment, loss, or suffering, I see you. And, more importantly, *God sees you*. He has never left you, even in times when you may have lost sight of him. But listen to me, and please press these words close to your heart: those people you love so dearly—*God loves them too*. And he hasn't stopped fighting for them either. Friend, I can tell you this: while reconciliation may not always be possible, peace is. My prayer for you is that you find peace in him by surrendering what you can't control, even if it means taking a safe step back to protect and care for yourself. You are allowed to have a better life than the one that was handed to you, and you are worthy of healthy relationships that reflect and honor all the beautiful ways in which he designed us to love.

ACKNOWLEDGE & CONFRONT

1. Is there a relationship that you have yet to grieve? Explain.
2. Is there an area in your life that felt broken, and God put it back together in a way more beautiful than before? Describe it.
3. Are you expecting your relationships to keep you happy, or are they "workrooms" for transforming you to be more like Christ?
4. Consider the legacy you hope to leave. What will others miss about you once you are gone?
5. Have you been waiting for an apology, changed behavior, or reconciliation with someone before pursuing freedom and healing right now in Christ? Explain.

Notes

Chapter 1

1. Theology of Work Project, "God Sets Limits," Bible Gateway, 2014, https://www.biblegateway.com/resources/theology-of-work/god-sets -limits-genesis-2-3-2-17.
2. *Encyclopaedia Britannica Online*, s.v. "Satan," accessed March 3, 2022, https://www.britannica.com/topic/Satan.
3. Charles H. Spurgeon, *The Gospel of the Kingdom: A Popular Exposition of the Gospel According to Matthew* (London: Passmore and Alabaster, 1893), 15.
4. *Encyclopaedia Britannica Online*, s.v. "Satan."

Chapter 2

1. Brené Brown, *Braving the Wilderness: The Quest for True Belonging and the Courage to Stand Alone* (New York: Random House, 2017), 136.
2. Kenneth L. Barker and John R. Kohlenberger III, *The Expositor's Bible Commentary—Abridged Edition: New Testament* (Grand Rapids, MI: Zondervan, 1994).
3. Sharon Martin, "The Enmeshed Family System: What It Is and How to Break Free," PsychCentral, May 3, 2019, https://psychcentral.com /blog/imperfect/2019/05/the-enmeshed-family-system-what-it-is-and -how-to-break-free#Commons-signs-and-symptoms-of-enmeshment.

Chapter 3

1. Caroline Knapp, *Drinking: A Love Story* (New York: Bantam Dell, 2005), 89.

Chapter 5

1. Lisa Whittle, email newsletter, September 2, 2022.
2. Thomas L. Constable, *Dr. Constable's Expository Notes*, s.v. "Jeremiah 29," StudyLight, accessed March 22, 2023, https://www.studylight .org/commentaries/eng/dcc/jeremiah-29.html.
3. Leo R. Sandy, "Good Families Aren't Born, They Are Made," Plymouth State University, accessed March 22, 2023, http://jupiter .plymouth.edu/~lsandy/healthy_family.html.

Chapter 6

1. Melody Beattie, *The New Codependency* (New York: Simon & Schuster, 2009), 42.

Chapter 7

1. "Signs of Resentment," WebMD, accessed March 22, 2023, https:// www.webmd.com/mental-health/signs-resentment.
2. *Merriam-Webster Unabridged*, s.v. "resentment."
3. Crystal Skinner, "Learning to Let Go of Frustration," Brighton Natural Health Centre, August 11, 2021, https:// brightonnaturalhealthcentre.org.uk/learning-to-let-go-of-frustration/.

Chapter 8

1. Henry Cloud (@drhenrycloudofficial), Instagram post, September 7, 2022.

Chapter 9

1. Lysa TerKeurst, "When It May Be Time to Draw a Healthy Boundary," Proverbs 31 Ministries, September 6, 2022, https:// proverbs31.org/read/devotions/full-post/2022/09/06/when-it-may-be -time-to-draw-a-healthy-boundary.
2. David S. Thompson et al., "The Right Kind of Conflict Leads to

Better Products," *Harvard Business Review*, December 23, 2016, https://hbr.org/2016/12/the-right-kind-of-conflict-leads-to-better-products.

Chapter 10

1. Salvador Minuchin, *Families & Family Therapy* (Cambridge, MA: Harvard University Press, 1974).

2. Jen Wilkin, "Developing Muscle Memory," video, part of the *God of Deliverance Bible Study*, Lifeway, accessed March 22, 2023, https://www.lifeway.com/en/product-family/god-of-deliverance-bible-study?playlistVideoId=6249414092001.

3. Craig Groeschel, Facebook, January 23, 2021, https://www.facebook.com/craiggroeschel/photos/a.119436738114919/3777691278956095/?type=3.

Chapter 11

1. Stephen B. Karpman, "The New Drama Triangles," USATAA/ITAA conference lecture worksheet, August 11, 2007, https://karpmandramatriangle.com/pdf/thenewdramatriangles.pdf.

2. Caroline Leaf, "You Are Not a Victim of Your Biology!," Dr. Leaf (website), October 3, 2018, https://drleaf.com/blogs/news/you-are-not-a-victim-of-your-biology.

3. Bible Hub, s.v. "4998 sóphrón," accessed March 22, 2023, https://biblehub.com/greek/4998.htm.

4. Lisa Bevere, Facebook, January 12, 2023, https://www.facebook.com/lisabevere.page/posts/pfbid035hAKtEWAfvmnmkTYrHuZyZ3EntwMvX8xoH6dyFZCKjEAAG4jRDHCtQsSFzZ6FvGNl.

5. Thanks, Sarah G., for this encouragement when I needed it most.

Chapter 12

1. NASCAR, "Twenty NASCAR Terms You Need to Know," accessed March 22, 2023, https://www.nascar.com/news-media/2017/08/01/news-media/twenty-nascar-terms-you-need-to-know/.

2. Brené Brown, *Daring Greatly: How the Courage to Be Vulnerable Transforms the Way We Live, Love, Parent, and Lead* (New York: Avery, 2015), 34.

3. *Merriam-Webster Online*, s.v. "litmus test," https://www.merriam-webster.com/dictionary/litmus%20test#learn-more.

Chapter 13

1. Henry Cloud, "Are You Carrying Someone Else's Knapsack?," *Boundaries* (blog), March 7, 2022, https://www.boundariesbooks.com/blogs/boundaries-blog/are-you-carrying-someone-elses-knapsack.
2. Will Guidara, *Unreasonable Hospitality: The Remarkable Power of Giving People More Than They Expect* (New York: Optimism Press, 2022), 5.

Chapter 14

1. "How Box Breathing Can Help You Destress," Cleveland Clinic, August 17, 2021, https://health.clevelandclinic.org/box-breathing-benefits/.
2. Blue Letter Bible, s.v. "G5424" (phren), https://www.blueletterbible.org/lexicon/g5424/kjv/tr/0-1/.
3. Joyce Meyer, "Knowing Who I Am in Christ," Joyce Meyer Ministries, accessed March 22, 2023, https://joycemeyer.org/everydayanswers/ea-teachings/knowing-who-i-am-in-christ. Emphasis added.

Chapter 15

1. "Sea Turtle FAQs," Loggerhead Marinelife Center, accessed March 22, 2023, https://marinelife.org/seaturtles/facts/.
2. "Life of a Loggerhead," Sea Turtle Patrol, accessed March 22, 2023, https://www.seaturtlepatrolhhi.org/life-of-a-loggerhead.
3. "Loggerhead Turtle," NOAA Fisheries, https://www.fisheries.noaa.gov/species/loggerhead-turtle.
4. Kelsey Huseth and Ally Thompson, "Reproduction and Life History," University of Wisconsin–La Crosse student project website, accessed March 22, 2023, http://bioweb.uwlax.edu/bio203/f2013/huseth_kels/reproduction.htm.
5. "Sea Turtle FAQ," Florida Fish and Wildlife Conservation Commission, accessed March 22, 2023, https://myfwc.com/research/wildlife/sea-turtles/florida/faq/.

6. *Encyclopaedia Britannica Online*, s.v. "kintsugi," accessed March 3, 2022, https://www.britannica.com/art/kintsugi-ceramics.
7. Paul David Tripp, *New Morning Mercies: A Daily Gospel Devotional* (Wheaton, IL: Crossway, 2014), 11.

Acknowledgments

I WANT TO THANK:

My husband, for loving me enough to tell me no.

Cheryl, for giving me a soft space to land in early sobriety and long after.

Sarah, for encouraging me to climb out of the crab bucket.

Dave, for making my work both better and fun.

Denise and Mattie, for introducing me to the team at W.

Stephanie, for believing in this new writer.

Brightman, for reminding me that this book and its timing has always been God's.

Melissa and my Generation Church family, for your mentorship and friendship.

My children, for breaking my heart wide open.

God, for your gracious guidance on how to love within safe limits.

Thank you.

About the Author

COURTNEY BURG IS THE FOUNDER OF DISCOVER
Your Worth, an online membership for women that offers coursework to help members heal from codependency and establish a boundary practice. She has her bachelor's in psychology from the University of Florida and is actively pursuing her master's in evangelism and leadership through the Propel cohort at Wheaton College. She and her husband, Jim, live in South Florida with their four young children.